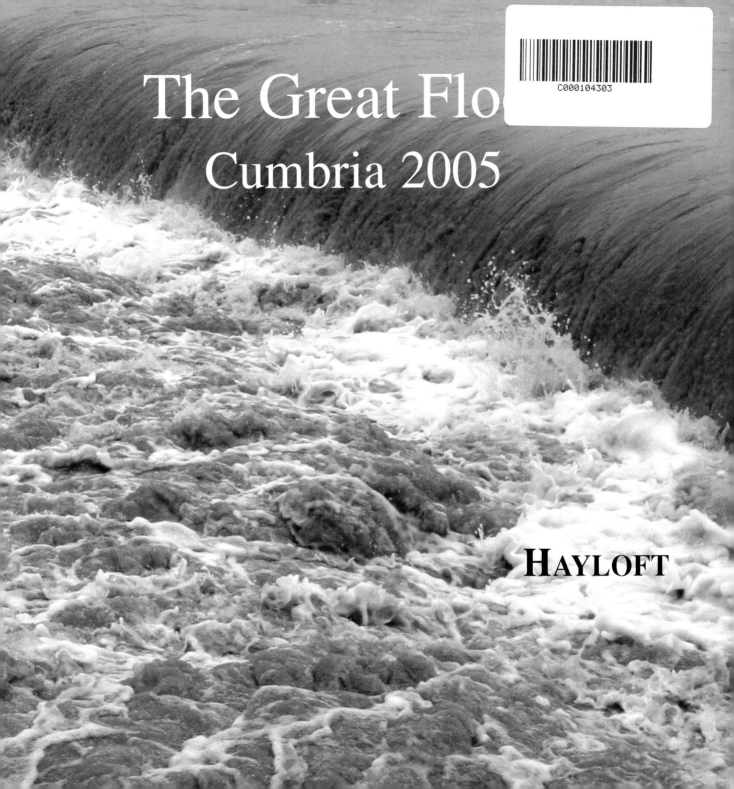

The Great Flood
Cumbria 2005

HAYLOFT

First published 2005

Hayloft Publishing Ltd, Kirkby Stephen,
Cumbria, CA17 4DJ

tel: (017683) 42300
fax. (017683) 41568
e-mail: books@hayloft.org.uk
web: www.hayloft.org.uk

ISBN 1 904524 28 1

A catalogue record for this book is available
from the British Library

Produced, printed and bound in the EU

This book is dedicated to the people of Cumbria.

Above, the River Eamont in flood near Penrith, photo. Peter Koronka.

Contents

Acknowledgements

We would like to thank everyone who was kind enough to spare the time to talk to us and to be photographed and all those who have helped make this book possible.

In addition we would like to say a special thank you to: BBC Radio Cumbria and their website at: www.bbc.co.uk/cumbria; Keith Sutton and Cumbrian Newspapers - the *Cumberland News* and the *News & Star*; *The Cumberland & Westmorland Herald*; *The Westmorland Gazette*; *The Westmorland Messenger*; *The Newcastle Journal*; *The Times*; Jeff and Olly Gibson; Martyn Boak; Trevor and Maryck Holloway; Ann Butler and Steve Weatherill; Kenneth Turner; Anton Hodge; Marie Dickens; Fred Wilson; Peter Cockshott; Patricia Howe; Phil and Pat Jones; Peter Longworth and David Jamison; Derek Gove.

Everyone in Cumbria has a story to tell about the floods and the storm and I wish it had been possible to speak to every one of them. This book is just a small sample of what happened.

Dawn Robertson, February 2005

The River Caldew at Holme Head, photo. Kenny Turner.

Facing page, the view across to Stainton from the Hadrian's Wall path, photo. Trevor Holloway

Introduction

Thousands of people were homeless and five people were dead after the worst storms in living memory battered northern areas in the early hours of Saturday, 8 January 2005. Carlisle was the worst hit with three people dead, including two elderly women neighbours on Warwick Road, who had sadly drowned in their homes and a man who was killed when a barn blew onto his caravan. Two men died when they were washed away by swollen rivers - one in Scotland and one in Yorkshire.

At Cairnryan, Dumfries and Galloway, on the west coast of Scotland a P&O ferry, the *European Highlander*, with a hundred people on board was blown onto rocks by hurricane force winds. Luckily no one died in this incident but only a few days later, Scotland bore the brunt of the continued storms and five people from the same family were killed on South Uist.

Emergency services in Carlisle were stretched to the limit to cope with the disastrous floods which engulfed the city. A flotilla of small boats, including RNLI inshore lifeboats, canoes and holiday dinghies, helped rescue people from their flooded homes. The boats were assisted by RAF helicopters, police underwater units, firefighters, mountain and cave rescue teams and an army of volunteers.

It was the worst flood the city had ever seen and an estimated 4,500 homes, schools and businesses in Carlisle were deluged. Around 10,000 people found

their homes cold, dark, flooded and impossible to stay in and were rescued and taken to reception shelters or went to stay with friends and relatives. The area immediately south of the River Eden was worst affected, especially Warwick Road, Denton Holme, Caldewgate, Hardwicke Circus and Rickergate.

The floods were caused by a massive cloudburst which dropped the equivalent of two months rain in 24 hours on Saturday. This was in addition to exceptional rainfall which had fallen on the county between Wednesday 5th January and Saturday the 8th. At Shap 227mm (nine inches) of rain fell in 72 hours of which 120mm (nearly five inches) fell on Friday alone. In addition to these exceptional amounts of rain, it had been wet and windy since the beginning of the month and fields and fells across the county were completely waterlogged and unable to soak up any more rain.

Every drop of water which falls on the Eden Valley, north Lakes and northern Pennines has to pass through Carlisle which has three rivers - the Eden, the Caldew and the Petteril. These were full to bursting and the situation was made worse by a high tide in the Solway. The circumstances of the day meant that the water had nowhere to go except into the city and, once it came over the flood defences, nothing could stop it. From 3am on Saturday morning the flood water rose inexorably and by early afternoon the flood peaked. In some places the water rose about four feet in one hour. Roads, normally busy with traffic, were turned into rivers, with only the tops of cars visible. Houses were up to six feet deep in water and everything was floating around.

Apart from the water from the rivers, the drains were also flooding, unable to cope with the quantity of water. Muddy brown river water was contaminated by water from sewers and with fuel from flooded cars and garages. Everything that came in contact with the filthy water had to be thrown away and police warned people to keep away from contaminated water if at all possible.

The Environment Agency later confirmed that flooding in the city was worse than the previous record flood of 1822. Some parts of the city were swamped in up to fifteen feet of water. The city's police and fire stations and the civic centre were flooded to a depth of eight feet, hampering the emergency services in their attempts to help everyone else.

Photographs on these pages, Martyn Boak.

To add to the flooding and storm damage, almost all homes in the county had no electricity so televisions, the internet and mobile telephones didn't work. Many telephone land lines were also cut due to the flooding. This almost total communication black out made everything worse. However, BBC Radio Cumbria was a light in the darkness as people in the county were kept informed by the heroic efforts of a handful of broadcasters.

The storm, which was described as a 'weather bomb', came only four years after the devastating foot and mouth epidemic which hit Cumbria so hard. No part of the county escaped the winds, which were in excess of 100 miles an hour, and the torrential rain. Buildings in exposed areas shook with the force of the terrifying wind. At the radar station on Great Dunn Fell a wind speed of 128 miles an hour was recorded. Across the region there was severe flooding, fallen trees, storm damage to houses and power cuts. In places the River Eden was recorded as being three feet deeper than it had been in the last great flood of 1968.

In Appleby homes and businesses were flooded on the Sands, Chapel Street and Bridge Street. The new flood defences held but the water was said to be only about two inches from the top of the barriers and some residents had to be evacuated.

A little further down the river at Bolton, near Appleby, the Butterworth family watched in horror as caravans from their caravan park were smashed by the force of the floods. At Langwathby the 'temporary' bridge to replace the one washed away in the flood of 1968 held, but a huge section of the road was washed away. At Lazonby the bridge was damaged and the road had to be closed.

Across the county more than half a million trees

The River Eden in spate from Wetheral Viaduct, photo. Anton Hodge.

had fallen. The Lake District did not escape the devastation. In Keswick the River Derwent broke its banks causing severe flooding in homes, shops and business premises. Hundreds of people had to be evacuated. There was flooding at other places too, including Pooley Bridge and Ambleside.

Homes at Corbridge were flooded and in Hexham the power of the River Tyne washed away a water mains, leaving the town without a water supply. In the Scottish borders there was flooding in Dumfries and in Kelso, where the River Tweed burst its banks. At Hawick the road was closed by a landslide.

The west coast of the county was battered by the hurricane force storms which left a trail of devastation, especially in Whitehaven and in Cockermouth, where many trees were blown down. Every country road in Cumbria was covered in a tangle of trees, branches and twigs. Many roads were still flooded two days after the storm.

Sadly cattle and sheep were drowned on farmland near the main rivers and wildlife too took a severe battering. A cormorant, normally only seen by the sea, was flying over Appleby looking lost - it had been blown fifty miles inland.

Ninety per cent of schools in the county were closed on Monday 10 January, either because of flooding, storm damage or because they had no electricity. A few schools faced much longer periods of disruption because of severe flood damage.

Carlisle MP Eric Martlew remembers the floods of 1968 and of 1983. He said that the flood of 2005 was a 'freak situation' and the worst ever to hit the city. Mr Martlew's home was flooded too so he knew how his constituents felt. He said: 'The Dunkirk spirit has come out but people get tired and cold by the third night without heating or electricity.'

Environment minister, Elliot Morley, visited the city to see the damage for himself. Mr Morley said: 'Climate change has got to be a priority globally because it is a reality.' He also said there would have to be 'substantial investment' in flood defences and warning schemes. He promised that the Government would meet about four-fifths of the cost of the clean up and that the Government would be reviewing the national flood warning system.

His Royal Highness the Prince of Wales visited the city on Friday 14 January to meet householders in Warwick Road and to see the damage at the civic centre, police and fire stations in Rickergate. By this stage some 800 homes were still without power but people were beginning to come to terms with what had happened.

The damage caused by the floods and hurricane was expected to run to tens of millions of pounds in Carlisle alone. One man said: 'What do you do when your life has been chucked out on the street for the bin men to collect?'

Another man said: 'Everything is nothing, and nothing is everything.' The sentiment summed up how people felt in the aftermath - depressed and tearful at the devastation to their homes and irreplaceable possessions and, at the same time, glad to be alive, safe and well, especially when they compared their fate to the hundreds of thousands killed or displaced by the tsunami in the Indian Ocean.

Photo. Peter Longworth

The Rescue Operation

As gales battered the county and huge amounts of rain fell from the sky, many people slept, unaware of the danger creeping through the city. Emergency services and the Environment Agency were keeping a watchful eye on the growing flood but no one imagined how bad it would get. As the night wore on the scale of the disaster became apparent and the automated emergency flood warning system began telephoning people to warn them of the encroaching floods. This was in the middle of the night, when most people were asleep - some did not hear the telephone ringing, others, confused by having just woken up, didn't act as quickly as they might have done and yet others did not receive the warning call because the automated system could not cope with the speed and scale of the flooding. Those who did receive a warning desperately tried to reach electricity meters to switch off the power and then tried to move precious items upstairs.

Meanwhile, as the grey light of dawn spread over the city, the heavy

Silloth Street, looking towards Hawick Street, photo, Trevor Holloway.

rain continued and rivers were struggling more and more to cope with the amount of water hurtling towards the Solway. Emergency services realised that the worst was yet to come and put out an appeal on local radio for anyone with a boat to come to help with the evacuation. Speedboats, RNLI inshore lifeboats, canoes, holiday dinghies, rowing boats - all started to arrive in the city. Coastguard teams from Burgh by Sands, Maryport, Workington, Millom and Walney answered the call and arrived in Carlisle to help as the rivers spilled out over the city. Coastguard teams rescued hundreds of residents including people in the Willow Park area as the Caldew overflowed. The teams also rescued two pregnant women, a man with broken ribs and a number of disabled people.

Carlisle Canoe Club members helped evacuate Corporation Road and Rickergate and around 500 homes in Warwick Road were also evacuated by boat. A veritable army of ordinary people helped the emergency services in the rescue attempt.

Two Sea King helicopters - one from RAF Bulmer in Northumberland and another from the Navy - were called in to assist with the growing emergency. Their main priority was to search for people trapped in isolated farms or buildings close to swollen rivers. One helicopter rescued an elderly man who had just had a hip operation and took him to the Cumberland Infirmary. Helicopters airlifted a further fifteen families from the rooftops of their homes. The RAF helicopter rescued two men who were stranded on top of a cement lorry for five hours. The water was up to the top of the windows of the lorry and the men were very cold but otherwise unharmed. Rescue boats could not get close to the lorry because of powerful currents. The RAF helicopter's crew included local man Mark Stevens, from Barrow-in-Furness, who is a radio operator.

Olwyn Gibson from Sandsfield Park, Carlisle, said: 'Mid-morning my husband, Jeff, and I walked into Carlisle in our wellies and waterproofs to see if we could be of help. We met a friend on the way who said the emergency services on Warwick Road were looking for volunteers. Jeff, along with many other volunteers, spent all day helping evacuate the residents of Warwick Road in the boats which people had brought down for the emergency services to use. There were boats with outboards, some with oars and

Photo, Jeff Gibson.

Everyone rescued from a house on Corporation Road, including the family dog, photos. Jeff Gibson.

some were being pulled along by people walking in the chest-high water - people were absolutely amazing.

'Some of the residents said they didn't want to come out of their homes and were settling upstairs for the night - during the day the sun was shining - but then as dusk arrived it became apparent that it wasn't going to be pleasant sitting upstairs in a cold, dark, damp house. There was no light or heating and many people then decided that perhaps it would be a better idea to be evacuated. This meant that the evacuations were being carried out in the dark - vehicles were parked with their headlamps on to give the boats some light, otherwise they were working in an eerie darkness.

'On Sunday Jeff and I took flasks of coffee, soup, etc., down to Warwick Road and I transported some of those who had stayed at home overnight to one of the evacuation centres in Edgehill Road. These people were, understandably, extremely cold and hungry, but the evacuation centres were well equipped to look after them.

'It really was a surreal situation all weekend. We, along with so many other people felt so helpless. We did what we could because we were in a position to do so - we had no dependents at home and we felt useless at home. It was obvious that there were many other people like us - the camaraderie was truly amazing and Radio Cumbria's coverage was second to none - it was a life line to many of those affected.'

At the height of the flood twelve families of showground workers had to clamber onto the top of their lorries from where they were rescued. Around 25 staff were also rescued from the McVitie's factory. A police underwater unit was involved in the rescue efforts along with mountain and cave rescue teams, all working against the odds to get people out of their cold and flooded homes. In all around 10,000 people were evacuated from their homes in the city.

People who were ill, disabled, elderly or very young, were obviously at most risk. The elderly and disabled had to be carried downstairs or rescued through bedroom windows. As all electricity supplies to the city were cut, homes became increasingly cold and people were unable to have hot drinks or food to warm them up. Mobile phones stopped working because of the power cuts and there was no news from television or the internet for the same reason. In addition many telephone land lines were down so people had to shout to the rescuers to let them know they were there. Some people were trapped in their homes for more than 24 hours without heat or power as rescuers worked around the clock to reach all those affected.

Peter Blythe, from Raffles, who runs All Seasons Groundworks, had gone to check that his mother was alright in Weardale Road. He then helped the rescue operation in the Caldewgate area. He said, in an interview with the *Cumberland News*: 'I went down with a rubber boat and there was a guy with a half tonne boat. He was on his own and he couldn't launch it. I assisted him in that and we got stuck together as a team all day. I don't even know his name! We were rescuing people and taking them to the Jovial Sailor pub. We were lifting them into the boat from the water - on most of them the water was at chest height. We didn't have any radio contact with the helicopter. It was all done visually by me and the pilot.' Among those he rescued were a three day old baby from the Maltings and a van on its way to the Willowholme electricity substation.

PC Richard Edwards, 33, rescued a man and his

Looking down Peter Street, to the fire station, photo, Jeff Gibson.

ing just under the surface of the water.

'I stuffed a tablet into his mouth and shook him round to make sure it had gone down. Thankfully he started to come to about 20 minutes later. He was then rescued by paramedics in a boat. I was just glad to get him out.'

Another tricky rescue was in West Tower Street where firefighters Andy Steele and Adrian Kevern

wife from their home in the Willowholme area which was six feet under water. The man suffered from diabetes and his partner from asthma. The man's medicine had been washed away. PC Edwards said: 'I tried to get him into the rescue boat but he collapsed straight into the water. I dragged him back upstairs and waited with him while his wife was taken away.

'It was an hour before they could get back to us. Because he'd not had his medicine he was going into a coma. He managed to tell me he'd last put it in the kitchen, and I waded through the flood water to search for it. Luckily I found the foil wrapper float-

and others helped rescue a woman who needed medicine and had to be guided out onto a ladder balanced in a boat. Fireman also rescued an 82-year-old woman in the Corporation Road area. They had to smash her bedroom window in order to free her. In some places downstairs doors were completely covered by water and it was very difficult to open them because of the weight of water pushing against them. Once firefighters had rescued people they were taken from the boats and handed over to police officers who were helping them to find shelter.

Tracy wrote on the BBC Radio Cumbria website: 'I was among about 70 guests at a 50th birthday party on Friday night in the Railway Club, Harraby. We were stranded by the rapidly rising water at Lady Guildford's bridge. As I am disabled I could not follow the valiant police officers who were leading people out in groups over the pedestrian bridge across the railway and into the cemetery at Upperby. They arranged for four fantastic firemen (who I later discovered had left their fire station in Wigton under a foot of water) to carry me on a chair over the bridge. They had already waded through waist high water to get to us and there were many slips, trips and stops in the pouring rain and gale force winds at 1.30am before we reached the other side... I have nothing but praise and thanks to everyone involved in helping me that night. Without them I do not know what I would have done.'

Bill Taylor said: 'I was involved in the evacuation of residents from Victoria Road and Tilbrock Avenue using a small dingy and was amazed by the spirit and even humour of the people having to leave their homes.'

An anonymous 'proud mum' on the BBC Radio Cumbria website wrote: 'Jason Rome and Nigel Millar of Harraby went with two boats early on Saturday morning and worked rescuing people on Warwick Road and Victoria Road until well after

Warwick Road, photo, Jeff Gibson.

dark, along with other boat owners. The water was freezing and fast running and full of diesel from the Esso garage. They had to avoid fully submerged cars, metal railings and a floating skip. They had to lift the two policemen in and out of the boats, plus the rescued people, pets and belongings. The water was nearly at the top of front doors in places... One of the policemen even rescued his own aunt.'

The following story is from the *Journal:* A family caught up in the floods were finally brought to dry land after spending 30 hours holed up inside their home in Warwick Road. Linda Hendrie and her two sons, Graeme and David, were confined to the first floor of their home when water engulfed the build-ing. They were rescued with their cat, Saatchi, in a dinghy.

Linda, who works for the NHS, said: 'The water was rising at a pretty constant rate, but then it suddenly shot up very quickly. We were stuck from about 10am on Saturday. We managed to get some food and it's not been too bad. The most worrying thing was not being able to contact anybody, or find out what was going on. Mobile phones weren't working and we had no electricity or phone lines.'

The following story is from the *Cumberland & Westmorland Herald* dated 15 January 2005: Two students from Penrith's University of Lancashire's Newton Rigg college rescued around 30 people from

Looking down Warwick Road from St. Aidan's Church, photo, Ann Butler and Steve Weatherill

Caldewgate, photo. Kenny Turner.

their homes. Eben Farnworth (21) and Russ Craig (20), both in their final year of studying for degrees in outdoor leadership, are both trained in river and water rescue. They took two canoes to the city on Saturday morning and were first on the scene in Warwick Road. The canoes were tied together and proved very mobile. Russ said: 'It could go anywhere with six inches of water or more. They said the water was getting high but I didn't think it would be that bad. I have driven down Warwick Road many times and to see it under water was amazing.'

Eben said: 'We thought on our way through to Carlisle that we wouldn't have to rescue anyone. I have never seen anything like it.' The pair rescued people from Charlotte Terrace and Warwick Road, including a three-month-old baby. They worked alongside members of Penrith mountain rescue team and with mountain rescue teams from Cheshire and Merseyside.

The following story is from the *Cumberland News*, 14 January 2005: A group of families and neighbours on Housteads Road in Sandsfield Park rescued dozens of people from houses and cars using a borrowed boat, liaising with emergency services and sustaining victims with hot food and drinks provided despite having no electricity in their homes.

The families worked for ten hours at Caldewgate and Warwick Road. The people involved were: Peter and Paula Campbell and their eldest daughter Laura (12) who is a pupil at Trinity School, plus neighbours Darren Brown, Ian Adams and Ashley Wilson.

They heard the appeal for boats on CFM first and couldn't believe it. Then they saw the appeal again on Sky TV at around 11am on Saturday.

Darren, who runs a roofing business, is a keen fisherman and has a small boat. Peter and Paula Campbell rang him and they then rang the police and were asked to report to Willowholme. When they got

Caldewgate, photo. Kenny Turner.

there the scene that met them was frightening. Paula said: 'The water came up so quickly. It was horrendous. Cars were starting to float. In 40 minutes water went from the bottom of the door of the Jovial Sailor to filling the pub.'

Darren donned his waders and spent the best part of the next ten hours up to his chest in the freezing, polluted, water. He pulled the boat and made many trips backwards and forwards to get staff out of the McVitie's building, helped by Ian, Ashley and Peter. Darren said: 'I just couldn't believe the amount of water. We got the double doors open and we got the boat almost in the building and were taking people off the stairs. There was a lot of petrol and grease in the water. It was awful. It smelled funny. I felt so sorry for the people.'

Other people were stuck in the Curry Master at John Street. Paula got into the boat and went to help them. She said: 'I didn't think twice. I can walk, I can talk, I can give out blankets. I just couldn't sit there. The people in the Curry Master had thought they were safe but the water was rising so fast it was covering the full shop window.' The rescuers used ladders from the nearby Joiner's Arms to help get people out of the curry restaurant.

By this time the current was getting stronger and they realised they needed a motor for the boat and petrol to fuel it. Meanwhile back at Housteads Road, the rescuers' families were waiting in the cold, without power, and worrying. Darren's wife Leanne, who was looking after their two children, Abby and Nathan, set out to try to find a filling station with electricity which could give her some petrol. There was no petrol to be had so they ended up having to siphon it from Ashley's car to get the boat's motor running.

With the help of other neighbours, Jim and Irene Maleney, Paula used her gas cooker to fill flasks with boiling water. She also rounded up chocolate biscuits and other snacks and went back to the floods and served food from the back of her car.

Once Caldewgate was evacuated the team moved to Warwick Road. Paula said: 'From the Botcherby end onto Warwick Road the water was very strong and was dragging the boats back to the river. We reported to Greystone Road where there were still a lot of people in their houses. When we got there Darren pulled and pushed that boat for about four hours. He must have rescued 50 or 55 people, maybe more. All the lads were absolutely exhausted when they came home.'

Paula and daughter Laura helped hand out food and hot drinks. Some of the firefighters and mountain rescue people had been there since 8.30am and had nothing to eat or drink. Paula said: 'A lot of people at the dry end of Greystone Road started refilling our flasks. It was absolutely amazing. It's often said that if there was another world war people wouldn't be communal or pull together, but we've always had a good community spirit.'

Twelve-year-old Laura said: 'I was a bit frightened of the water. In McVitie's there was an electricity box and they didn't know if it had been turned off. We were taking people off the boat and they were saying they were cold and their houses were wrecked... I was worried about my dad. When they went out on the boat looking for people I was worried they weren't coming back.'

The Housteads team finally went home at around 9pm. Darren said: 'I was absolutely exhausted. I had cramps from wading through water all day. Going against the current, it was

really strong. I don't think I could have gone on much longer.'

Rescuer Ian Adams said: 'It was sad. Many of those people didn't have insurance. People were putting on a brave face but a lot were shocked. A lot of people we took on the boat just couldn't believe what was happening to them. It was strange. We just didn't know what to say to them... The water was freezing. One of the official rescue teams said don't go in without proper protection because of hypothermia, but there were people in the water in shorts and tracksuit bottoms.' Ian's wife Andrea was looking

Caldcotes (McVitie's) roundabout from Wigton Road, photo. Trevor Holloway.

Corporation Road, photo. Kenny Turner.

after their children, daughter Eden aged four and son Lewis aged nine. Lewis was terrified he might not see his dad alive again.

The following story was in the *Cumberland News*, 14 January 2005: Wigton solicitor and boating enthusiast John Hawks, from Newby Cross, near Carlisle, was one of those who answered the call to help. He rescued more than 80 people from the Willowholme and Caldewgate areas, with his sixteen-foot motorboat. He was woken at 5am by the hurricane force winds which tore tiles from his roof. He switched on his radio and heard reports of the devastation caused by the storm and, at 8am, the police appeal for boat owners to help stranded residents. An hour later he was launching his boat into the water that covered Caldewgate.

John said: 'It was an incredible sight. The road had just disappeared under the water. The keep-left signs at the roundabout were completely submerged, and the water was up Port Road.'

In the coming hours he worked with the Globe pub's landlord Steven Dixon and Caldew Electrical Supplies boss Kevin Winter. The local men's knowledge was invaluable in helping to avoid underwater obstacles.

First they rescued residents from Willowholme,

including a small group stranded in a caravan. John then took his boat to the White Arrow Express haulage depot. John said: 'We found five or six shift workers there: they'd jumped into some kind of container - I think it was a skip, which was floating in the loading bay. They had to duck their heads to get out under the door.

'Further along the road, we found a man in a temporary office building, and he was in real danger. The whole thing was almost completely under water, and he was submerged up to his armpits, and cling-ing to the doorway. The current was very strong. The firefighters used lines to rescue him. It must have been very frightening for him. The firemen gave him instructions, roped him up, and pulled him into the boat, soaking wet and freezing cold.'

John also led rescues in the Rigg Street area of Caldewgate including families, five dogs and several pensioners. The most difficult rescue was that of an elderly woman who was recovering from a broken leg. John said: 'Four firemen broke into her house, waded in, and then had to tear off a wardrobe door to

Rickergate, photo. Peter Longworth.

Left, Port Road (!) and the Jovial Sailor, looking down Caldcotes towards McVitie's, photo. David Jamison.

Below, Paddy's Market and John Street with Shaddon Mill in the background, photo. Peter Longworth.

use as a stretcher. They put her on to it and carried her out, keeping her above the flood. We'd made a bed with cushions for her on one side of the boat. She was wrapped up in curtains and blankets. She was great, but very cold. We took her up to Port Road, hoping there would be an ambulance for her, but then commandeered a van to take her up to the hospital. That all took 45 minutes. We also took a manager from McVitie's into the factory where workers were stranded. We took out a boat-load of them.

'Later, United Utilities brought in a big truck, which they drove down Wigton Road and into the flood. It didn't get far - it ground to a halt in six or seven feet of water. We had to rescue five of them through a window of the truck.'

An RAF helicopter winchman asked John to rescue a family with a three-day-old baby from The Maltings as the RAF team did not want to risk lifting the baby into the helicopter. John said: 'We rescued the parents, the baby, and their other child - a four-year-old boy. The current there was really strong. It all seemed totally unreal. At the time, it seemed like a bad Hollywood disaster movie - a little bit over the top. It didn't seem real.

'We just got on with it. All of the people I was

Shaddongate, photo. Kenny Turner.

working with - the fire crews, Steven, Kevin, and another man called Pete whose second name I didn't get - were heroes. I remember thinking how odd it was that this was all happening in the middle of Carlisle... It's only afterwards that the danger of the situation comes home to you.'

As well as rescuing people, many dogs, cats and other pets were rescued. One person was said to have forgotten to pick up their kitten. Rescuers went back to collect the animal and found it still fast asleep on the sofa, which was floating around the living room.

As evening drew closer the evacuations continued. People who had stayed in their homes until this point began to think again as the reality of a night in the dark, damp and cold, with no food or means of communication, began to sink in. Coastguard volunteers visited all the houses along Warwick Road and advised people to evacuate their homes. Homes that had been checked were marked with tape to show others members of the emergency services that they were empty.

Those who decided to brave the night in their own homes were visited throughout the night by members of the emergency services and volunteers in boats. The only light was from torches carried in the boats and an occasional candle in a bedroom window and the only sound that of lapping water in the streets.

Sadly, despite the heroic efforts of the emergency services and so many volunteers, two elderly ladies died as the floods engulfed their homes in Warwick Road. They were Margaret Threlkeld who was 78 and her 85-year-old next door neighbour, Margaret Porter. They were found by horrified rescuers. The

Looking down Victoria Road onto Warwick Road, photo. Ann Butler and Steve Weatherill.

Caldewgate, photo, Kenny Turner.

ladies were neighbours and friends and are thought to have died at about the same time, unable to summon help from those in the street outside.

Their bodies were discovered as the floods went down on Sunday morning. Police said that a post mortem revealed that drowning was the cause of death. The fate of the two pensioners put into perspective the trauma of hundreds of people made homeless by the flooding.

Neighbour, Shirley Cockburn, said: 'It is an awful tragedy for two old ladies to lose their lives in those conditions. They were both very pleasant and knew each other well because they had lived next to each other for years and years.

'Miss Threlkeld was a spinster and had difficulty getting around - I think she was more or less house-bound. Mrs Porter was a widow and suffered from osteoporosis. She was tiny but very sprightly and did as much as she could.

'When the water came, it rose very quickly and I suppose they just couldn't get out in time. There was a young lad with a boat in the street and he went in

to try to find them. At first he couldn't find Miss Threlkeld. It was when he went in for the second time that he found her body. We have all lost a lot through this but it is really sad that these poor people lost their lives.'

Debenhams and Warwick Street from Castle Way, photo, Jeff Gibson.

Flood facts

The freak weather which hit the north was a 'weather bomb' - so named because the storm arrived so suddenly and with such force. A massive cloudburst dropped the equivalent of two months rain in just 24 hours on the Saturday of the flood. The rain that had fallen on the Eden Valley and surrounding areas for the three days before that had been exceptional. At Shap 227mm (nine inches) of rain fell in 72 hours, almost double the January average of five inches. In fact 120mm (nearly five inches) fell on Friday alone. Keswick, which also experienced severe flooding, recorded 137mm (5.4 inches) in 72 hours, with 95mm (3.8 inches) on Friday 7th January. According to meteorologists, the rain was caused by a stream of warm, wet, south-westerly winds coming from the sub-tropical Atlantic. The winds were forced to climb over the

The River Petteril had gone down by Monday morning but was still almost touching Botcherby Bridge, photo. Peter Koronka.

mountains of northern Britain where they deposited their rain.

This amount of rain, by itself, was enough to cause severe flooding, but two other factors made things worse. There had been steady rain for the previous three weeks, leaving fields sodden and unable to soak up any more water. In addition there was a high tide in the Solway, leaving nowhere for the water from the Eden, Petteril and Caldew to go.

The Lake District is well known as the wettest place in the country but it has an efficient system of rivers to carry huge amounts of water from the mountains to the sea. The Rivers Kent and Lune flow into Morecambe Bay. The Esk and the Derwent

The River Eamont which runs from Ullswater to the River Eden burst its banks and flooded fields near Brougham Castle. The force and sheer amount of water brought all sorts of debris with it including a gas canister and many trees. Every drop of water which falls on the Eden Valley or northern Lake District has to pass through Carlisle on its way to the sea, photo. Peter Koronka.

The River Eden near Tesco's - the river is actually behind the bank in the distance, photo. Peter Koronka.

flow directly into the Irish Sea and the Eden flows through Carlisle to the Solway Firth. The River Eden drains the northern Pennines and the west of the Lake District. Usually only one side of the catchment area, or the other, suffers heavy rain so the system can cope, but this time the whole region had exceptionally high rainfall. For 99 per cent of the time the rivers work perfectly but extreme weather and human interference can make the rivers fail.

The flood of January 2005 was soon confirmed as higher than the worst flood ever recorded in Carlisle, in 1822. Water marks left under the Eden Bridges, showed the level of the 1822 flood, and could be compared with the level of the recent flood. It was also confirmed that the 2005 flood was around one metre (more than three feet) higher and caused much more damage than that 37 years before in 1968.

The River Eden reached its peak in the city at around 3.45pm and then slowly the water began to recede. At the peak of the flood the Environment Agency recorded water flows in excess of 1,500 tonnes per second at Eden Bridges. The previous record, from the flood of 1968, was 1,300 tonnes per second.

Many people believe that freak storms such as the one that hit Carlisle or Boscastle, are the result of

global warming and that severe weather and flooding could become a fact of life if climate change continues. Environment Agency flood defence manager Ian Hodge said: 'Climate change is about increased storminess and intense short rainfall and we expect to see more of this.'

The Times weatherman Paul Simons said that extreme weather has happened since time immemorial. However all the recent extremes fit into a pattern which suggests that experts' predictions about climate change are true. He wrote: 'Our winters are milder and wetter, with rainfall coming in heavier downpours, and we may be turning much stormier as well.'

In the summer of 2004 in the Canadian Arctic, the Inuit were amazed to find a wasp - they had never

The River Eden looking east towards Willowholme Industrial Estate, photo. Trevor Holloway.

seen one and had to be warned not to touch it. Simons goes on to say that the Arctic ice is melting so fast that within 50 years it may be possible for ships to sail across the north of Canada and Russia. The Alps are defrosting and crumbling as their permanently frozen ice-caps melt, causing serious rock falls and Mount Kilimanjaro, in Kenya, is expected to lose its snow cap within 20 years because it is melting so fast. Simons argues that the world is getting wetter as well as warmer as more water evaporates from the oceans and flood disasters have been increasing since the 1950s.

People also expressed the theory that the storm which hit Cumbria was somehow linked to the Asian tsunami disaster which killed three hundred thousand people, including approximately 400 from the UK. Experts said that the Boxing Day tsunami was caused by the biggest earthquake for decades and was so powerful that it shifted the whole planet by 2.5 centimetres.

An Environment Agency spokeswoman said: 'Climate change is a fact. It is a reality. The events of this weekend will of course be used to inform our decision (about flood defences) and we will aim to provide the most appropriate level of protection for the homes and businesses at risk.'

In a report in the *Cumberland News*, Environment Agency area manager, Kim Nicholson, said: 'You can never guarantee to people that it won't flood. What you can do is defend against it as much as possible and manage the risk. You can't build flood barriers across roads and barriers won't stop water coming up

The River Caldew at Mill Race, Denton Holme, photo. Peter Longworth.

33

The disused railway bridge over the River Eden, west of Willowholme, photo. Trevor Holloway.

through drains, as happened in Carlisle. Just because it was a once-in-200-years flood doesn't mean it will be 199 years before it happens again. It could be any time. The climate is changing in ways that challenge our previous assumptions.

'Droughts are becoming more common, winters are becoming wetter. In the past year we've had summer floodings in Boscastle and winter floods in Carlisle. They are not similar but they were both caused by intense rainfall.'

The Environment Agency had predicted the areas of the city most vulnerable to flooding and had invited residents to take part in an automated early warning scheme which would warn them of high water levels. During the Carlisle flood not everyone received a warning. An Environment Agency spokesman said that the flood warning scheme did not work perfectly because the Agency monitor rivers and much of the water came from other sources such as over-flowing drains, sewers and the tons of water which fell on the city.

Following the devastating floods, experts such as Ian Gregg, chairman of the National Association of Rivers Trusts, and the Eden Rivers Trust, were quick to point out that human interference has made the flood situation worse. There were three main points:

1) Large areas of the uplands have been drained for the benefit of grouse and sheep. These areas used to act like giant sponges, soaking up heavy rainfall and then releasing it slowly back into the river system.

2) Up to 80 per cent of the traditional wetlands on the Eden and its tributaries, have been drained to provide better grazing land since the 1950s. These areas also help to absorb heavy rainfall and then slowly release the water back into the river system.

3) Disappearance of flood plains due to building - water can soak into grassland but it

Above, the River Caldew at Denton Holme, looking towards Maryport Cottages, photo. Peter Longworth.

Left, the torrential downpour which blocked drains and contributed to the flooding in Carlisle, photo. David Jamison.

just runs off tarmac, increasing the scale of any flood. There has been extensive building close to the Eden, some on the flood plain itself. Planners, the Environment Agency and builders are often at loggerheads over building projects near to rivers.

Carlisle's existing flood defences were strengthened after the flood of 1968 and had been effective up until now. However on the Saturday of the flood, the water level at 2.45pm was three feet higher than the man made barriers along the Eden, Caldew and Petteril rivers.

The Environment Agency already had plans for a £20 million increased flood defence around Carlisle. These plans were out for public consultation with work expected to start in 2006. However, in the light of the floods of 2005, the Environment Agency will be reconsidering the plans to see if a larger scheme should be built. Options include raising the height of the existing defences and creating flood water storage areas. There are also plans to negotiate with farmers to return areas of flood plain back to their natural state with open water features and wetlands.

The Government said it would support the city's bid for improved flood defences. The Government has also reported that spending on flood defences must rise by £30 million a year for the rest of the century, a 20-fold increase, to tackle global warming issues.

The River Caldew at Denton Holme, photo., Kenny Turner.

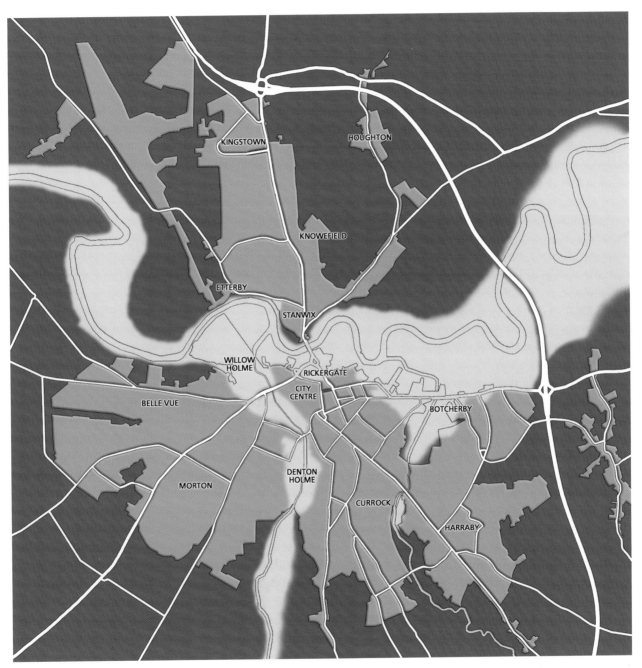

The areas of Carlisle reported to have been flooded by the Rivers Eden, Caldew and Petteril are highlighted in light blue. Graphics by Derek Gove.

Freak weather facts, from *The Times*, Thursday, 13 January 2005:

Record breakers:

- 2004 was the fourth hottest year worldwide on record. Ten of the warmest years on record have happened since 1990.
- Iceland's highest temperature on record (24.8C) was recorded on 11 August 2004.
- Weather cost the insurance industry £18.5bn in 2004, an unprecedented amount.

Freak winds:

- First hurricane in South Atlantic in March 2004. Five cyclones in Arabian Sea in 2004.
- There were 1,717 tornados in the US in 2004, breaking the previous record of 1,424 in 1998.
- Tropical Atlantic sea surface temperatures have steadily risen since 2000 which might explain unusual hurricanes.

Stormy weather:

- There were eight tropical storms and hurricanes in the Atlantic in 2004, setting a new record.
- First recorded tropical storm of 2003 in the North Atlantic formed in April 2003 - the season normally begins in June.

Snowfall:

- Saudi Arabia had big snowfalls in January 2005; 2004 saw snowstorms in Lebanon, Israel, Greece and Turkey.
- Texas had record snows at the end of December 2004 and had its first white Christmas in 86 years.

Rainfall:

- Major floods struck China, the Philippines, Japan, Kenya, Namibia, Mexico, Nicaragua, Siberia, Hungary, Bosnia, Papua New Guinea, Fiji, New Zealand and Australia.
- The Sahara had extraordinary rains in 2003, leading to a massive plague of locusts in West and North Africa in 2004 which even reached Italy.

Drought:

- In 2004 there were droughts in western US, parts of Africa, Afghanistan, Australia, parts of China and India.
- In Australia the January to July rainfall 2004 total is the second lowest on record. Driest autumn since records began in 1859.

UK:

- The temperature record was broken at Brogdale, near Faversham, reaching 38.5C on 10 August 2003.
- The first ten months of 2003 were the driest since records began in 1766. In Scotland the air became as dry as the Sahara with only two per cent humidity.
- In Boscastle, Cornwall, a total of 75mm of rain fell in two hours one Monday in August.
- Snow disappeared in the Highlands - for only the fourth time on record.

The emergency services

The most incredible thing about the emergency services in Carlisle on the weekend of the flood was that they were so amazingly brave, efficient and organised, despite the devastation to their own headquarters by the floods. It was the biggest emergency operation Cumbria had ever faced and the emergency services knew they only had a few hours to rescue thousands of people. They were stretched to the very limit but somehow managed to organise a flotilla of small craft and a safe evacuation.

The city's police and fire stations in Rickergate were swamped by up to eight feet of water. Police officers were evacuated early on Saturday morning when water began to seep through the back of the station. Ten minutes later it was two feet deep. The 150 uniformed officers who normally work from the station moved to a mobile station near Marks & Spencer in the city centre and later to some former

An ambulance caught in the floods in Denton Street, photo. Kenny Turner.

Photo. Peter Longworth.

Carlisle Police Station, photo. Ann Butler and
Steve Weatherill

county council offices in English Street. CID and other specialist units, such as the Child and Adult Protection Unit, moved to other buildings belonging to the police force.

The following story appeared in *The Journal* on 11 January 2005: 'Inspector Adrian Sowerby assessed the damage - files of vital evidence, court exhibits and CID files were among the debris in the dirty water. He said: 'It is going to take some time before we can even assess the amount of damage caused here...

'Certainly the place is in a mess. Walls have collapsed and exhibits and court files have disappeared under water. But I'm sure they can be rescued. They will dry and life will return to normal.'

Meanwhile Insp. Sowerby was directing traffic on a roundabout near the police station when the river burst its banks. He said: 'I was standing there watching as the water spilled over a wall and started pouring towards me. Within 30 minutes I was up to my knees and it was rising fast. What has impressed everyone about this is the spirit shown by the people of Carlisle.'

During the emergency Cumbria police received three times as many calls as usual from members of the public. There were on average 14,000 calls a day to the control room at the Carleton Hall police headquarters near Penrith. The HQ building itself did not

Carlisle Police Station, photo. David Jamison.

escape damage with some flooding and a power failure.

Police officers from across the county went to Carlisle to help with the disaster. Off-duty officers and special constables also volunteered to help and extra uniforms, radios and torches were sent from Penrith. As well as rescuing stranded residents, the police also set up road blocks on flooded roads into the city and set up a gird in order to check every house affected by the floods.

Chief Constable Michael Baxter wrote in the *Cumberland News* on 13 January 2005:

'I would like to express my appreciation and admiration for the efforts of everyone who played a part in responding to Cumbria's floods.

'That includes the emergency services, the voluntary agencies who receive and deal with those affected, those working in difficult conditions to restore power and particularly to individuals and communities who not only helped us but helped themselves and each other.

'The list of those who contributed is endless and the identity of many who helped in some way may never be known. This emergency has demonstrated the capacity and the spirit of Cumbria to deal with a crisis of this scale. I wish to express my sincere appreciation to everyone involved in this difficult time for their efforts...

'The Cumbria Constabulary is the primary and leading agency in co-ordinating an emergency response and management of major events and incidents, until such time as the local authorities are in a position to manage recovery from that event.

'The past five days, particularly the weekend period, have seen extraordinary demands placed upon the force and other emergency services because of the severe adverse weather and its effects across the county.

'The loss off Carlisle police station so early in the emergency added to the difficulty in responding to

Carlisle Police Station, photo. Peter Longworth.

The Fire Station in Warwick Street, photo. Kenny Turner.

events as they unfolded in North Cumbria.

'Nonetheless, an emergency response to prevent loss of life in the first instance and then to look after people's well-being was accomplished in difficult and extreme circumstances.

'We are all now looking to see how we can recover from this unique event and I hope we work as well in that recovery as we did in the critical incident management of it.'

The community spirit of 99.9% of people in Carlisle was much praised but there were a few who took advantage of the situation and started looting. Thieves raided builders' merchants in the city during the power cuts and stole up to £80,000 of machinery and in another incident a newsagents in Newtown Road was broken into. Extra police were drafted in to help with the problem of looters and they were also warning residents about bogus builders who were taking advantage of the misery.

James Ratcliffe wrote on the BBC Radio Cumbria website: 'After being stranded in the city centre in my car, I had to leave my car and wade through three feet of water to get home. On the Sunday I found my car broken into and missing a radio. I was gutted. My thoughts go out to people who lost their homes and had their homes broken into.'

Next door to the police station, the city's firefighters were also flooded out and had to move up to the emergency centre at Carlisle Castle. The *Cumberland News* reported that firefighter Martin Ogilvy left Carlisle Fire Station in Rickergate at 8.15am to buy a newspaper on Scotch Street. When he returned half an hour later, his work place and the next door police station had been consumed by eight feet of filthy water.

The fire service control room in Cockermouth had to prioritise 999 calls as there were so many and resources from all over the county were sent into Carlisle as the scale of the disaster there became

Bicycles behind the police station. One of the back walls of the station which housed an administration office was demolished by the force of the water, photo. Peter Koronka.

The police station was off limits to all visitors following the floods as the building was dangerous. The photograph shows the high-tide mark on the front of the police station and cars left where they had floated away, photo. Peter Koronka.

apparent. Local crews were joined by volunteer colleagues from Merseyside and Cheshire.

The fire service performed a major part in the rescue operation across the county and were called out to countless emergencies. They worked hard to rescue people from flooded homes and vehicles. The service also gave advice to people, especially on the fire danger caused by electrical systems which have been flooded. On Saturday morning exactly this scenario arose and the flood waters shorted the electricity supply in a house in Peter Street causing a fire. Firemen were called to rescue people from upstairs rooms thick with smoke.

With evacuations going on all night, the emergency services brought in earth-moving equipment to open the banks of the Eden in an attempt to prevent further

Left, a fire engine waits while firefighters take a boat down Greystone Road to rescue stranded people, photo. Marie Dickens.

Below, the city's fire station under water, photo. Peter Longworth.

devastation.

Firemen worked one shift after another to tackle the problems during and after the storm. Some worked for 24 hours without stopping, fuelled by adrenaline. Firefighters helped pump out houses, moved valuables upstairs and rescued people whose cars were stuck in the floods. Five young people were rescued from a car which was stuck in water on the Pooley Bridge road. On Saturday morning, to add to the difficulties, there was a four vehicle crash on the M6 to which the emergency services were called.

A fire service spokesman said: 'All the vehicles parked in the yard behind the station were ruined by about four feet of water. We're getting rid of ruined kit and cleaning up.' The station doors were damaged when water got into the

Carlisle's Fire Station, photo. David Jamison.

electronics and office computers, paperwork and furniture were being thrown into skips.

Soon after the floods had subsided Carlisle firefighters tested brand new pumps worth more than £2 million which had been brought in by the government as part of the Civil Resilience Programme following the 9/11 disaster. Nine of the high volume pumping units, which have never been used in the UK before, were used to help lower water levels at the Hardwicke Circus underpass and at the Willowholme estate to help the city get back to normal. The pumps carried some eight thousand litres of water per minute back into the river.

The Cumberland Infirmary cancelled all non-emergency operations because of the power cuts. The hospital was able to use generators and continued to treat emergency cases and urgent operations. Around 120 people were treated at the hospital over the weekend for injuries or illness related to the flooding. Some patients were transferred by air ambulance to the West Cumberland Hospital in Whitehaven.

By Tuesday the Cumberland Infirmary was continuing with all normal operations and radiotherapy treatment. Doctors' surgeries were re-opened even

Above, Paul Bates and Steven Berwick from Aspatria were helping with the clean up at Carlisle Fire Station.

Left, vehicles damaged by the flood at Carlisle's Fire Station, Photos. Peter Koronka.

though some did not have power. Many day care centres were closed because power cuts or flooding.

At Keswick Hospital the power was off and the floods were threatening the building so staff decided to transfer patients to Penrith Hospital.

The ambulance service struggled to reach people in emergency situations because of the floods and roads blocked by fallen trees. Two air ambulances were scrambled from their bases in Teeside and Blyth to help the emergency services in Cumbria. The helicopters, operated by the Great North Air Ambulance charity, helped transport people to hospital when ambulances could not get through the floods. They also flew patients from the Cumberland Infirmary in Carlisle to the West Cumberland Hospital in Whitehaven after power cuts affected some treatments.

Mountain rescue teams helped the emergency services in the rescue

Two officers from the Child and Adult Protection Unit who were busy moving furniture from rooms above the police station to a temporary office at Longtown. Though the upstairs offices were not damaged by water, there was no electricity or heating in the building, photo. Peter Koronka.

operation. Penrith team members used telephone boxes in Scotland Road where they used radio links to provide emergency response cover. The Patterdale team brought a boat to the city to help with the evacuation.

Officials from the fire and ambulance services, the Environment Agency, United Utilities, mountain rescue teams and local councils were all at Cumbria Police's headquarters at Carleton Hall, Penrith. They were in constant contact with the emergency planning team at Carlisle Castle. The operation to save lives was called 'Gold Command' and lasted for three days and was then handed over to the council.

One of the country's top military officers, Major General Euan Loudon, was flown to Carlisle Castle by helicopter on Monday to visit servicemen and women based in the city. Twenty RAF personnel from Spadeadam and eight soldiers from the 37 Signals regiment were in the city to help with handing out food and supply parcels. The Major General toured the county's Emergency Planning HQ at Carlisle Castle where police, fire and council officers were based during the floods. Major General Loudon said: 'It's absolutely staggering. It is hard to believe how high the water has been in some places. In the brief time I've been here I can see that the spirit of helpfulness between people is magnificent. Everyone seems to be pulling together.' Major General Loudon commands the Army's 2nd Division in Scotland and the north of England.

Photo. David Jamison.

Some personal stories

Residents of Tilbury Road were badly hit by the floods and several of them were at Valerie Thomson's house as she was able to make hot drinks on her gas cooker. Jo Simmons, who was seen being rescued on Sky TV, said: 'I felt a bit stupid being taken away in a dinghy. I can swim and I had tried to walk out at first but I didn't realise how cold the water would be. It was freezing so I came back to the house.' By 1pm on Saturday the water was about three feet deep and even deeper at the far end of Tilbury Road. The water came up so quickly and when people realised that they had to get out it was hard to think of everything. In one case a pet rabbit was drowned. Aline Lataix who is from the Auvergne region of France said: 'I didn't know my neighbours but I know everyone in the street now. It's brought us all together.'

Valerie Thomson said: 'I was rescued with my dog who had to swim along to the boat. He's now in kennels. My son said I should go because there was no power and no heat. I have been so much luckier than some. I had a premonition on Friday night. I

Valerie Thomson, Michelle Howie and Aline Lataix, photo. Peter Koronka.

didn't go to bed and they rang me at quarter to four in the morning. Some friends came to help and we carried things upstairs. My car was in the garage and it started first time. I'd left the radio on and the song that was playing was *Land of Hope and Glory*!'

Valerie was cooking for the whole street on her gas cooker as the electricity was off from about 11am on Saturday morning. She said: 'The water came up so quickly. There was nothing here at 6am but by 8.30am there was three feet of water at the end of the street. The bathroom had flooded and a bottle of domestos had floated up onto the mantlepiece. There was nothing you could do and even freezers were floating.'

Michelle Howie escaped out of the back of her house. She said: 'I jumped into the water and it was absolutely freezing and I only got about quarter of the way through. It was so cold we had to come back and we waited here and got out in the end.'

Mr and Mrs Wright from Wood Street had some flooding and had no electricity. Mr Wright said: 'No one's been round to tell us anything.' Their carpets were damaged and the freezer contents had defrosted. They were using candles for lighting. Mr Wright added: 'The thing that I'm going to complain about is that there was no warning that it was coming in the next half an hour. We had a letter about it and I filled in a card saying we wanted to be warned but there was nothing whatsoever. Perhaps they thought it would not go over. It was freak weather.'

Mrs Wright said: 'We feel like tramps and things are very difficult. We've got no radio and it was quite scary because we had no warning. We have a friend with a severe heart condition and he had water up to

Mr & Mrs Wright, photo. Peter Koronka.

two feet deep. It must have been frightening. We are doing his shopping. He's got to keep warm but he can't because there's no heating. We've been boiling water up in pans for him and filling hot water bottles for him. The police were using dinghies up and down this road. We think it might have something to do with the tsunami and the world's got knocked off its axis.'

Mrs Wilson who lives in Warwick Road said: 'The water was about two feet deep. My daughter, who lives in Scotby, insisted that I went to stay with her.' Her son Martin Wilson who lives in Glasgow had come down to help clear up and was throwing out the carpets. He was trying to get hold of the insurance company and said: 'We're going to have to make lists of things that are damaged. It's just a horrible mess.' Mrs Wilson said: 'They did ring me at about 4am on Saturday morning to say there was a liability of flooding. Some of my neighbours were very distressed.' Mrs Wilson's daughter and son-in-law have a factory near the River Caldew and have had a lot of damage. Looking on the bright side Mrs Wilson said: 'At least the car started and it doesn't normally start!'

Joe and Sandie Grieves of Warwick Road said the water started coming into their house at around 3.30am. Sandie said: 'It was coming in at the back and the front of the house and in the end it was about four feet six inches deep and was up six stairs. We only had fifteen minutes warning and we just did not

Joe and Sandie Grieves, photo. Peter Koronka.

have time to get things upstairs. It came that quick and we couldn't carry the sand bags. We didn't manage to switch the electricity off and by the time it was starting to come up the stairs the electricity was sparking. There was petrol and diesel floating on the water and the phone wasn't working so we couldn't get in touch with anyone to help us. When it got to the window bottoms we left in a boat. Our son's supposed to be doing exams but it's impossible. We can't get the electricity back on and it's so cold, especially at night. It's damp, wet and cold.'

Hundreds of video tapes had to be thrown away along with irreplaceable family photographs, some dating back to the 19th century. Joe had a massive collection of old comics from the 1960s, and rare military books - again all ruined. Joe said: 'We can't touch anything until the assessor comes round. We can't get batteries or candles as the shops have run out.' Sandie added: 'Where do we start? It's a Catch 22 situation.' Christmas presents were ruined and they felt cut off because they couldn't get any information and angry that they only had fifteen minutes warning.

Despite the chaos of their own situation the couple were helping their neighbours with hot water. They came back to the house because of the threat of looting. Sandie said: 'We have lived here seven years and we have never seen it flood over. It came round the back of the houses and up Warwick Road and it stopped at the traffic lights. The authorities were coming past with a motor boat and a rowing boat asking if we were OK. Because we could not see it stopping rising we asked them to take us to the traffic lights but there was nowhere organised to put people at that time.' Joe said: 'I had been in the water and by the time I got back I was shaking with cold. That

Odd items lying in the street, left by the flood, photo. Peter Koronka.

including the CD collection. She said: 'It's been awful. I've been getting shopping for people but when you go to the shops you have to have cash to get things because the tills aren't working.'

Mr Foster from Warwick Road said: 'We had a call at 3.15am on Saturday to say there was a severe flood warning and to get things upstairs. I looked out of the window and there was already a river out on the

Mr Foster and daughter Amy, photo. Peter Koronka.

water was really cold and I was trying to get the electricity off. It feels surreal. We are in limbo and no one is giving us information. I would have thought there would be someone from the council round to tell us what to do. The emergency services did a great job though.' Carol Mills from Currock was helping the family cleaning anything she could street and then seven minutes later we had another telephone call telling us to move to higher ground, so we went upstairs! Later when there was about two feet of water some idiots with four wheel drives were going up and down and causing a wave which made even more water come into the houses. All the neighbours were helping each other. We are staying here because there are people out pinching stuff and I've heard that they've broken into various places up and down the road.'

Rory Cockshott, Warwick Road, said: 'I'm trying to dry the place out and get cleaned up. I don't trust these contract teams.' The back garden was still deep in water and under it was Rory's fish pond. He said: 'It was the deepest here of anywhere and people died on this road. I've never seen it like this before. We had five feet of water in here. You see it on TV but it's not the same as when it happens to you. But what can you do? You may as well laugh.'

Rory spent fifteen years in the Marines and said his military training took over in the emergency. He took photographs of the damage in his house and then set about clearing it up. By Monday lunchtime it was empty of furniture and carpets. The floors had

Looking up Warwick Road towards Brunton Park, photo. Steve Weatherill and Ann Butler.

been given a first scrub down and Rory was busy washing the crockery, every piece of which was covered in a layer of brown mud.

The water rose very quickly in his house, even coming up through the concrete floor. The kitchen

Above, Carlos Salvador, photo. Peter Cockshott.

Doreen Leask, pictured above, said: 'There's been lots of damage to the contents and the floors. I have two cats and my husband came to rescue me. It's just unbelievable. I couldn't believe it was happening and it was really scary. I stayed upstairs with my cats until we could be rescued.' Photo. Peter Koronka.

appliances were all brand new but were all ruined. Rory said: 'It was very disorientating because things were floating around and you didn't recognise your own house. There was even a dead fish in my kitchen. I cannot explain how cold the water was. We were absolutely numb. We all eventually got out of the place because you did not know when it would stop. We just waded out.'

Rory's son, Peter, said: 'I was amazed at how fast the water came up. There were cars just floating around in the street including a brand new Mini Cooper. Petrol and diesel, anything plastic, all sorts of things were floating about. I went all over the city taking photographs and I reckon there was almost fifteen metres of water in Hardwicke Circus and the water on the Carlisle United pitch was up to the top of the goal posts. It was like the Carlisle swimming pool'

Carlos Salvador said: 'Me and my wife were rescued in a boat. The lady next door had to be rescued too and she's seven months pregnant. The water came up three to four feet in less than two hours and I was very afraid. I was saying to the people in the boats, 'Please take the women and children first.' I was in the water and it was very, very, cold. It was so cold I lost the feeling in my legs.'

Carlos' car was parked near to Carlisle Football Club and was ruined by the flood. His car, like many, was still under water on Monday because once the water breached the flood banks it couldn't get back into the river and took days to drain away.

Rory said: 'I was staying out at Warwick Bridge and I heard about an elderly lady whose car was being washed away. Two men, I think they were Australians, saw what was happening and managed to get her out by smashing the sunroof.'

He continued: 'It was strange because there were TV people everywhere but they didn't realise that all our comms were not working. Mobiles wouldn't work but if you had an old style telephone with a wire they still worked if they were

Peter and Rory Cockshott and Carlos Salvador with Rory's ruined kitchen equipment in the background, photo. Peter Koronka.

Mrs Pauline Maud and Stephen Hogarth with their ruined possessions, photo. Peter Koronka.

upstairs. We did not see any of the TV coverage. This house was on page three of the *Sun* yesterday!'

A couple of weeks later, Peter said: 'Everyone's fine - just in the drying stage of the house, floorboards up, walls are back to brick, no plaster or anything, big industrial dryers and dehumidifiers everywhere.'

Ian Whelan, wrote on the BBC Radio Cumbria website: 'Carlisle simply looks like a war zone in places. The emergency services are doing a fantastic job, especially as the police and fire stations were both flooded... Living next to a river is idyllic most

of the year but on Friday night the roar of the River Caldew and the debris and damage it has caused in Denton Holme, were a sobering sight.

Another man escaped with only the clothes he was wearing and an electric guitar when his basement flat in Willowholme Gardens was completely submerged.

Andy Murray who runs 24Seven Ltd. which owns property in Warwick Road said: 'We didn't have any warning at all. It's been devastating at Crosby-on-Eden and here in our offices and flats. One of the tenants, Steve Cochran, had to be rescued. It's been

Left, Andy Murray clearing out ruined furniture.

Below, Gordon and Anthony Milburn were moving sodden carpets, mattresses and furniture out of some bedsits where ten people live. Mr. Milburn said: 'We're trying to get all the carpets up and things outside to let the building dry out.'

Photos. Peter Koronka.

a big tragedy but the information was nil. The only organisation which was giving us information was BBC Radio Cumbria. They were the best and I listened to it for two days. It was absolutely A1. That's where I got all my information from. The awful thing is that there are gangs of lads going round robbing places.'

One man told how he swam round his living room in his home in Corporation Road to rescue pictures off the walls. The water was coming up through the carpet in his home and at first he thought he'd left a tap on. When he looked out of the window he said it was like being in a goldfish bowl because the water was already half-way up the windows.

Seventy-eight-year-old Mr John Ayre lives above Struts shop in Dixon Street. His daughter Jayne Ivinson had a telephone call from Susan Ayre who works in the shop and also lives above it to say that the water was coming in. Jayne said: 'Susan was trying to lift computers off the floor but eventually she was so scared because the water was coming in so quickly that she left. I kept ringing my dad and his partner, Doris Rwan, to check they were alright. I was on the telephone to him all morning but nothing

Corporation Road, photo. Kenny Turner.

seemed to phase him at all. At about 2pm the water was hitting above the shop sign. It was just before the peak and they decided to bring him out. Someone climbed in the window - the boat was very wobbly - and he was lowered down with Doris. They were taken up to the Wigton Road Methodist Church where I went to see them. They were sitting at a table as if they were at a coffee morning. Doris said: 'We went through the Blitz!' The young people were more hysterical than they were. We have re-housed them for the time being with some relatives.' Jayne and her husband Anthony tried to get to Carlisle to help her father and Doris but they were stopped by

Left, John Ayre and below, precious belongings ruined by the filthy water lying on the street waiting for the rubbish collection. Photos. Peter Koronka.

floods every time. They finally got as far as Stanwix where they left the car and went on foot to Hardwicke Circus but they couldn't get any further. Jayne managed to tell the police about her father and they finally got the news that he and Doris had been rescued.

Photographer Paula Paisley is pictured below with a piano she was given as an engagement present by her nana. The piano will never play again. When the flood started, Paula was on assignment taking photographs for the *News and Star*. She said: 'My kids and my husband were stuck in here. When I left at 8.20am the water was up to the door step. I went to take pictures of Bitts Park. Of course later I could not get back - by then the water was up to my hips.'

Paula's husband Jonathan, who is a chef, and her children, Lewis who is four-years-old and Jos who is 18-months, were stranded in the house by the flood water and Paula watched as the emergency services rescued her family.

She said: 'At about 2pm the firemen had been over in boats and they started getting everyone out and they had to get them out of the upstairs window.' Many of the family's possessions, including books,

Paula Paisley, photo. Peter Koronka.

Corporation Road, photo. Jeff Gibson.

photographs and negatives from twelve years of Paula's work plus the laptop with its digital images were lost to the floods. Paula also lost her car which she had only bought four weeks before.

Paula and Jonathan and their two sons decided that they would have to move out for several months before their home is fit to live in. Paula and her family were filmed for a BBC One programme *Accidents Can Happen* which follows people after disaster has struck. The presenter is former *Eastenders* actress Nadia Sawalha. The house, like so many others, had to be checked by a structural engineer as floors were damaged and walls need re-plastering, decorating, plus new kitchen, bathroom and furniture.

City taxi driver and author, Marie Dickens said: 'We were worried about my great-aunt but then someone rang to say they'd seen her on Sky television being rescued so we knew she was alright and she's staying with us now. Our taxi company was affected because of the power cuts and because we couldn't get anywhere. It was interesting that when there were no traffic lights there were also no traffic jams. Finding that out was one of the only bonuses of the flood. People often say that there are too many traffic lights in Carlisle.'

Trevor Holloway who lives in Berkeley Grange, said: 'The first we knew about the flood was when a friend, Muriel, rang to ask if we were alright. She and her husband, Rod, live in Tebay and he'd been to Kendal that morning to a church meeting and had to move three trees to get there. They were on their way up to Scotland and saw the floods from the M6.

'We went down to the river and it was easily as wide as the River Loire. Seeing electricity pylons standing in water was a bit unnerving. We stood on the bank behind the hospital and looked over towards Willowholme. We could see the water flowing through the buildings. We went down towards Dixon's chimney until we couldn't get any further. There were still idiots trying to get through the floods in four wheel drive vehicles.

'On our way home we met one of our neighbours

Corporation Road area, photo. David Jamison.

Steven Gardner was staying at his sister's house in Sheffield Street and did not manage to rescue any of his possessions because he couldn't get back to move anything. He said: 'I've lost everything.' Photo. Peter Koronka.

whose husband is a police photographer. As I understand it, he had gone into work in the morning and then someone had gone in and said, 'I think you'd better move your cars.' He'd gone out and the car park was covered in water but he had to go back to get his keys. By the time he came back from getting his keys the water was half way up the car.

'What was most touching was at 6pm a friend of my wife, Maryck's, from Bordeaux rang to ask if we were alright, followed by her mum from Angers, and then friends in Ireland and Spain. They had heard about the flooding but in Carlisle it was almost a black out situation. If it hadn't been for Radio Cumbria and our battery radio we wouldn't have known anything.'

Maryck Holloway said: 'At first I was quite blasé about it. I'm used to seeing the countryside flooded, as I come from Angers on the River Loire. For me floods are par for the course. But when I saw the floods in the middle of the city it was awful and now, with all the furniture on the streets, it looks as though a bomb has gone off. It feels like a haunted place - it's wierd. But no doubt the people of Carlisle are resilient and things will get back to normal.'

Gavin Bowman, a freelance IT consultant, had been sleeping in at his home in Corporation Road on Saturday morning when his mobile phone rang. 'It turned out to be my mum, who'd heard about the rising water. But at the time I was so sleepy I just wandered downstairs without thinking.

'I didn't even notice the water. I just started thinking, 'Why are my feet wet?' At that stage it was up to my ankles, pouring in through the front door. I made a grab for my computer but it was already under water.

'I managed to get a few other things upstairs and was coming back down for more. But even in those few seconds they'd been washed away. We've lost virtually everything - computer gear, wedding photographs, the lot.'

Mr Angus Graham from Milbourne Street said: 'We were flooded out. It was about three and a half feet in the house and we have

Shaddongate, photo. Kenny Turner.

66

couldn't block the vents. Then we realised the carpet was soaking and we thought we'd better get the TV and other things lifted up. We only had about five minutes and then the carpets were floating. It was three and a half feet deep in just half an hour and the floorboards started lifting. We grabbed some food and the dog, Becky, and went upstairs.

Left, Willow Bank, River Caldew, and below, Caldew Maltings from Bridge Street, photos. Martyn Boak.

had to move to Gretna while the house is being done. It might be three to four months before we can get back in. We got a flood warning at about 3am. My wife Pat went to check and I got up at about 4am and looked out of the window and the street was like a river. It hadn't come into the house at that time and I went out just before 10am on Saturday morning. I was near the castle when Pat rang to say the water was coming back. I got back as quickly as I could and by that time it was a foot and a half deep. I'd got sandbags at the front door but I

Our feet were freezing because we'd been in the water.'

Angus and Pat stayed in their home and Angus said: 'Later on we were watching people on the street with torches checking houses. It was absolutely terrible.' Later on, when the water had receded, Pat had an accident and fell through the floorboards hurting her leg. Angus said: 'We were two hours in the accident and emergency ward on Tuesday.' He went on to praise the church in Milbourne Street which was giving people free cups of tea, coffee and soup.

Six-year-old Marcus from a village on the River Eden, near Carlisle, wrote the following account of the flood:

'Ten past five. AM. There's a strange noise coming from outside. I know it's windy but this sounds like something is broken. I am not scared though. The light is still on in the hall and it's too early to wake Mummy and Daddy up. I pull the covers over my head and try to go back to sleep. I don't need the toilet.

'Twenty minutes to six. AM. Someone is in the bathroom. It must be Daddy because Mummy will be too tired because she is having a baby soon. It is 37 weeks old now, but when it is born it will start again at zero. I go and stand outside the bathroom, waiting for him. He says good morning to me, but I can't see him because the light is shining in my eyes. He tells me he is getting up to look and see what the banging noise is and I follow him out to the front door. I need the toilet now, but I don't want to go in case I don't see the banging thing and I don't like being alone when some of the lights are not on yet, even if just for a second.

'Daddy opens the door and says a word that I don't know, but I think it must be an angry word. He puts

a coat on and rushes out to the car, where someone's bin is banging against the front, which is the engine part, and someone else's bin is banging against the side.

'Daddy isn't very angry though and he comes in and makes me some toast and a cup of tea. He tells me we can't go into town today because of the wind and the rain, but that's OK, I think, we can go in tomorrow. I am going to buy some more magnets with my Christmas money and go to the library with my book about earthquakes. They sent me a letter, and they need it back, because somebody else wants to read it. Mummy said that lots of other children wanted to know about earthquakes now after the

Greystone Road, Botcherby, photo. Martyn Boak.

Satsuma in Asia on Boxing Day, but Daddy said it was because I'd had the book for four months. But it's OK because children don't have to pay if they have books too long.

'Daddy is listening to the radio in the kitchen and I am watching Tom and Jerry on the cartoon channel. They are very funny, but not as good as the Simpsons. I tell Daddy that we can go into town tomorrow, but Daddy says that the magnets shop isn't open on Sundays, and I say we have to go into town today then. Daddy tells me that Carlisle has been flooded and that no cars can get through.

'Ten past ten. AM. Daddy switches on the internet computer and we see some photographs of boats in Carlisle sailing down Warwick Road. Some of the cars are covered in water. I am really annoyed. I tell Daddy we have to go on the motorway and the road which is near to Asda and he tells me we have to go and get some bread and milk from the garage in the village.

'We walk down the main road to the bottom, where the River Eden passes through the village, and when we get there there are lots of people. The road is covered in water and there is a fire engine stuck in it. My school is near there, but it is quite high up and there is no water in the playground, but the football pitches and the play park are like a lake. Daddy says that we should go and get Mummy and our digital cameras, so we have to walk all the way back up the hill. We stop at the garage. It looks closed, because there are no lights on, but we go inside. There are people inside looking for milk, but there is none left. Daddy gets some bread though and a bag of peanuts, but I don't like peanuts and Mummy is not allowed to eat peanuts because she is having a baby soon, so he buys chocolate bars for me and Mummy.

'When we got home, Mummy is up. I don't want to walk again, so I switch the TV on, but there is no picture and Mummy says that all the electricity has gone off.

'We all go down to the river again, and there is even more water. A man in a big high-up car wants to drive through it, but the fireman says he isn't allowed to. There is shouting. "You are not a policeman. You can't stop me," says the man. Then he gets into his car and drives through the water. I think the fireman will be angry, but he just smiles. The man's car stops and lots of people laugh and cheer. Me and Daddy do too, but I think it is a bit naughty. The man shouts for help, but no-one goes to him. Eventually he gets out of his car and wades through the water to the side of the road. The water goes up over his waist and his tie floats on the surface, pointing out in front of him. The firemen goes over to him and I think they become friends now.

Falcon Mews looking along Walkmill Crescent,
photo. Steve Weatherill and Ann Butler.

Photo. Martyn Boak.

them or anything like that. Daddy says we have to stop staring and anyway he tells me to look at the helicopter which is flying very low. My friend Blake is there and he says the helicopter is rescuing people, but when I look up, I can see the people in it have a camera and I think they are from the television.

'Sunday morning, I wake up at half past seven AM, and it is still a little bit dark. I switch on the light but nothing happens and I remember that there is no electricity. Mummy is up, but Daddy is still sleeping. We

'Even more people come down to see. Some of them say that they hope Mummy doesn't have the baby today. We take some photographs. The water has gone into some people's houses and they are trying to shovel it out. They let us go into their back gardens to see the water and they don't shout or cry or seem annoyed. One man has a little stream near his house and it is getting higher against his walls. A lot of people are looking at the wall and pointing and taking photographs and he seems angry with them, but he doesn't hit

View into Willow Park from the old St. Joseph's home, photo. Steve Weatherill and Ann Butler.

play some games of draughts and have some toast, but we have to cook it under the grill, as the toaster needs electricity, and it smells like we are cooking bacon and Daddy gets up and says he wants a bacon roll, but Mummy says we don't have any bacon or any rolls. She says she wants milk, so, at ten past ten AM, Daddy and I go in the car to look for some milk. When we go to the car, we notice that we now have FOUR bins! We have to go a funny way because the main road is still flooded and before we get to the motorway, Daddy stops and rings Grandad and Grandpa on his mobile phone to tell them that we are OK, but that we don't have any electricity or phones or milk.

'We drive on the motorway and because we live only 7 miles from the border we go to Scotland where Daddy says there will be milk. We go to Gretna where you can see the first house in Scotland and people wearing kilts. Beside the kilt shop there are some Highland Cattle, which are brown hairy cows with big horns that you only get in Scotland. I want to go and see the cattle, but Daddy says we need to go to the camping shop to get some gas for the lamp and some batteries for the radio. In Scotland all the electricity is on, although there were some floods there too. I think then that Scotland must be a better place to live and England is a rubbish place, but I don't want to change school, so we have to stay where we are. They also speak a different language in Scotland. I know some of the words, but not all of them.'

The following stories are just some of the many reported in the local newspapers. From the *Cumberland News:*

Mandy and David Pattinson were just getting used to life with their new born son, Aidan, when the flood

A dinghy left behind on Warwick Road after the evacuations, photo. Peter Koronka.

hit their home in Milbourne Street. The couple were asleep when they heard banging on their window. They thought it was drunken revellers but in fact it was the police trying to warn them of the impending flood. David, who works as a builder, sealed the doors of their home with silicone sealer when they realised the flood was coming and they moved electrical items upstairs but it was too late and by 11am on Saturday morning the entire street of 140 homes was swamped under four feet of water. David and Mandy could only watch as the water came in through air vents and up through the floor. Their home had been done up by David but sadly the couple weren't insured and faced huge losses.

The following story is from the *Journal:* Sammy Carter and her children 16-month-old Joseph and eight-year-old Leah, who lives with her partner Neil Irving, said the speed of the water rising was frightening. It filled the ground floor in just 15 or 20 minutes and was soon only two feet from the ground floor ceiling. The family escaped upstairs with whatever they could save. Sammy and Leah were rescued through a first floor window by volunteer rescuers in a rowing boat. She said: 'They were using the oars to push off the roofs of vans and cars to get down the street. It was absolutely terrifying. I just couldn't believe what was happening. I was desperately worried about the baby. It's frightening when you don't know when the waters will stop.' Neil and baby Joseph were picked up later by speedboat. The family were taken to a nearby Methodist Church.

Eric Dawes from Warwick Road rescued his 86-year-old deaf neighbour as the River Caldew flooded the area. Eric, who runs the Court Field B&B with his wife Marjorie, said he had heeded the severe weather warnings, but never expected the water to reach his home.

He said: 'My neighbour had fallen in the water, so I carried her on my back to my home. We thought we would get a brush to start cleaning out her home, but the water kept coming.

'In my house it's three feet high, but in the ground floor flats along the street you're looking at up to five feet of water, or more. It's incredible, and people have lost everything.'

Eric remembered the last time the Warwick Road area flooded in 1968, but said that 'did not compare' to the damage the floods had caused this time.

The following stories all appeared in the *News & Star:* Eric Guest who is registered blind, escaped from the flood with just his white stick and the clothes he was wearing. At first he thought the flood only affected his ground floor flat but when he opened the door the water came pouring in. He said: 'In a couple of minutes, it was waist high. I shouted for help and two lads came in and took me to an upstairs flat, where I spent the night. My flat is

Looking down St Aidan's Road, photo. Martyn Boak.

totally gone. All I've got are the clothes I'm standing in.'

Margaret and Melvyn Aitken were evacuated from their home in Warwick Road with their three children, Michael, Laura and Daniel, along with Mrs. Aitken's mother Alice Dalzell. The family were evacuated by boat at 9am on Sunday morning as the water rose to three feet deep. Margaret remembers the flood of 1968 when the water came to the top of their front step. She didn't think it could get as high as it did. She said: 'A lot of our neighbours have gone back to their homes. The people at the reception centre have been brilliant - they all come and talk to you, but there's nothing anybody can do. We'd rather be at home.'

Single mum Fiona Smith who has seven children, stayed at the Harraby centre with her three youngest - four-year-old Heidi, three-year-old JJ and one-year-old Angel who was suffering from a chest infection. Her four older children were staying elsewhere. The family left their home in Milbourne Street after the flood water came in,

Top, St. Aidan's Road looking towards the Stoney Holme Golf Course and below, taken from St. Aidan's Church, looking towards Warwick Road. Photos. Steve Weatherill and Ann Butler.

destroying much of their home. Fifteen-year-old Tanya lost all her schoolwork. Fiona said: 'We spent last night here and it feels like we'll be here forever. The house just doesn't look liveable. I was all right yesterday, but now I'm feeling weepy. I think I'm in shock.'

The following stories appeared in the *Cumberland & Westmorland Herald*: An 82-year-old Warcop man whose house was pumped out by firemen in the early hours of Saturday, said it was the worst flooding he had seen in the village.

Above, Walkmill Crescent.

Right, the view from Wood Street, looking towards Eastern Way, photos. Steve Weatherill and Ann Butler.

Neil Richardson, who lives at The Fox, with his wife, Margaret, and son, Joseph, said: 'I've never seen it so bad. Water was flowing in the back door and out the front.'

Water got into the ground floor of the house despite sandbags at the doors. All the ground floor carpets were ruined along with electrical equipment, including a washing machine and freezer.

Mrs Richardson praised the help they had received from friends and neighbours. She said: 'I've never seen the village like it. It was just one big lake and it came up so quickly.' The home of Les and Beth Baines, who live nearby was also flooded.

Ian Stevenson and his fiancée, Kath Woof, were in their home at Charlotte Terrace, off Warwick Road, when the area was flooded. A policeman alerted them to the danger of flooding at around 3.15am by which time the water was up to Mr Stevenson's knees when he went to get some sandbags. He and Miss Woof began moving their possessions upstairs and moved their cars to higher ground. By 4.30am the water was rising up the stairs of the house and tidal waves from lorries driving past made the situation worse. By 7am the couple were stuck upstairs. Mr Stevenson said: 'We just watched the water gradually rising. We were watching the stairs, counting how many steps we had left before it hit the bedroom. The worrying part was when it started lashing down. I looked outside and saw a caravan but by the time I had gone to have a look at the stairs and looked out again it had disappeared. It was quite frightening.'

Just after 12pm two Newton Rigg college students, Eben Farnworth and Russ Craig, arrived with two canoes tethered together and started to evacuate residents, including Mr Stevenson and Miss Woof. Mr Stevenson said: 'We have got out and all we have lost are a few possessions. We feel really lucky and we have got nothing to complain about when something like the tsunami has happened on the other side of the world.'

James Pittam and his girlfriend Rebecca Thorburn, who live at Thirlwell Avenue, off Warwick Road, also suffered flooding with water coming up to two or two and a half feet deep. Mr Pittam opted to stay at his property without electricity and heating until Sunday. He said: 'It was just surreal, as if it was a dream you just couldn't believe it.'

Shaddongate, photographs opposite page, David Jamison.

Business

Hundreds of businesses in Carlisle and across the county were affected by the floods which caused millions of pounds worth of damage. Some firms faced months of closure while the clean up went on and some even faced permanent closure. Businesses not affected by the floods were hit by power cuts and many had to close until electricity supplies were restored. Those that were open were lit by candles with calculators to do the adding up as electronic tills were not working. City centre shops were not directly affected by the flooding but on the Monday following the flood the city centre was like a ghost town as there were so few shoppers.

Cumbria Chamber of Commerce chief executive, Viv Dodd, said a meeting with business people affected by the floods was 'extremely traumatic' and 'some of the stories were horrific.' Repairs were

Foreways News, Food and Wine on Warwick Road had just been renovated and expanded before the flood - everything had to be thrown away because it was contaminated with flood water. Pictured above is the owner Bill Bone, photos. Peter Koronka.

The DFS furniture showroom near Hardwicke Circus lost all its stock, photo. Martyn Boak.

expected to run into millions of pounds and the Chamber was keen to point out that the city remained open for business despite the difficulties.

The Chamber of Commerce and organisations such as Business Link were offering help to try to sort out the problems as quickly as possible and Kingmoor Park Properties in Carlisle offered a month's free accommodation for businesses which had been forced out of their properties by flooding.

Foreways News, Food and Wine was just one of many businesses which were badly hit on Warwick Road. Bill and Jenny Bone were clearing out on Monday and everything was going into the skip as all the stock had been contaminated by filthy water. Bill said: 'We've just had the extension done and the lads

who are here helping are the builders. The water was four feet up the walls and all the food and beer has to be thrown out as it's contaminated.'

The Beehive Inn on Warwick Road was devastated - you can see the mud on the furniture and how it floated and ended up everywhere on the photographs over the page. The kitchen was perhaps worst hit with the freezers floating around and the cellar was still full of water three days after the flood. Landlord Michael Wheatley said: 'We had six feet of water in places and even deeper in the cellar. The water was well over the pool table. I left on Sunday afternoon

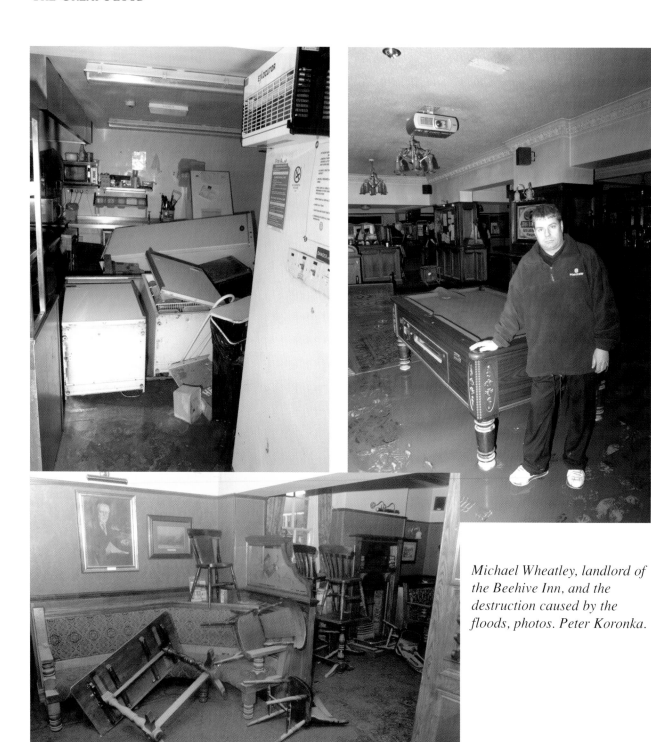

Michael Wheatley, landlord of the Beehive Inn, and the destruction caused by the floods, photos. Peter Koronka.

at about 1pm because I was fed up of the cold. In the kitchens all the freezers floated around. Six freezers full of food are ruined.'

Several garages were under water, including the Shell garage at Hardwicke Circus and the Esso garage on Warwick Road. On the weekend of the floods it was impossible

to get petrol in the city and it was feared that fuel would have leaked into the flood water from garages and vehicles.

Tesco's narrowly missed being flooded. The power cuts meant that the store had to dispose of all fresh and frozen food, leaving many shelves half-empty. During the floods staff found themselves cut off and unable to get home.

Top, Shell garage at Hardwicke Circus, photo. Jeff Gibson.

Middle, Shell garage at Hardwicke Circus, photo. Martyn Boak.

Bottom, Esso garage on Warwick Road, photo. Steve Weatherill and Ann Butler.

Strut's Fancy Dress in Dixon Street was dev-
astated, but owner Jayne Ivinson, (above) kept
cheerful, photos. Peter Koronka.

Strut's fancy dress shop in Dixon Street was devastated. Jayne Ivinson had been in business there for 22 years and she was trying to salvage what she could. She had collected special clothes many of which were antique and irreplaceable. The water was over their heads and almost up to the roof. Jayne said: 'We managed to get down here on Sunday with waders to see what had happened. On Hardwicke Circus we could see party poppers and things floating. Stuff was literally floating out of the door. We looked at the devastation - everything had floated away and been distributed. Now the water's gone down the stench is terrible. We are waiting for the insurance assessor - we just want to get rid of the filth. Sometimes you think it's all too much and then you think it's better to just get on with it. Some people have lost everything and we've lost a life time's work. We had some very special clothes, antiques we can never replace. We also had clothes and boots that had been worn by famous pop stars.'

The Italian Ristorante Adriano in Rickergate was devastated by the floods, photo. Peter Koronka.

Linton Tweeds Mill in Shaddongate was flooded and expensive knitwear was destroyed along with furniture and fabrics. The Milbourne Arms and the Knight Inn pubs were both flooded but, despite that, and a lack of electricity, both buildings became a refuge for local people who gathered in the candle-light to talk.

Bill Finlayson's hairdressing salon in Corporation Road was flooded. Bill said: 'I cracked up when I looked inside this spot, then I thought, hang on mate, you have walked down here, just get stuck in because there are thousands of other people who have had it worse than you. On the 2nd of January this year I celebrated 40 years of being in business and less than a

*Pictured top, left to right, Colin Harkness,
Christine Finlayson, Bill and Jean Finlayson.
Below, the pile of equipment from the shop.
Photos. Peter Koronka.*

McVitie's biscuit factory is Carlisle's biggest employer. Note the car in the picture above by Martyn Boak. By the time the picture below is taken by Jeff Gibson, it has almost disappeared - you can only just make out its roof.

THE GREAT FLOOD

Photographs these pages, David Jamison.

week later I'm out of business for a while."

His wife Jean and his business partner Christine who is a specialist in hair extensions, were helping with the clean up, along with Colin Harkness. Christine, who lives in Askerton Close, said: 'The water just seemed to wash through the property. All the chairs are in a big pile.'

McVitie's was forced to close its Caldewgate biscuit plant when flood water rushed through its bottom floor in the early hours of Saturday morning. Fortunately no one was injured but employees were left with an uncertain future, not knowing when, or even if, the factory would re-open. McVitie's promised that it would resume production as soon as possible. The biscuit-making plant in Caldewgate suf-

fered damage estimated at £1 million. The company, which was founded in 1831, is owned by United Biscuits. Ironically the first water biscuits were baked at the plant.

On the BBC Radio Cumbria website, Emma Duke wrote: 'Having left night shift at McVitie's I managed to walk home through the water which had come into the factory and then through the water on Junction Street which was up to my knees. On my arrival to my street, Bousteads Grassing, I found the water to be above my waist! I then somehow managed to fight my way through it all, with trees and branches, etc., which had been washed up off the River Caldew. I was so glad to get home safely.'

This page - the clean up operation at the McVitie's biscuit factory, Carlisle's largest employer, where 1,100 people work. It was a massive operation but the company said they had already got a 'recovery plan' in operation three days after the flood, photos. Peter Koronka

Left, Caldewgate from bottom of Shaddongate and below, Hardwicke Circus, photos, Peter Longworth.

The Gordon Box garage on Caldewgate was one of the businesses to suffer from the flooding, photo. Martyn Boak.

Other companies closed following the floods were Ali's Takeaway in Shaddongate, Babyland and Tumble in the Jungle, in West Tower Street and the Stony Holme and Swifts golf courses. Plus the Golden Pheasant and the Globe pubs, Suzuki KC

This bed & breakfast business and the Bed Centre, on Warwick Road, were both affected by the floods and storms.

Caldcotes, photo. Trevor Holloway.

Shaddongate, photo. Jeff Gibson.

Motorbikes and Elegant Bathrooms. The Used Furniture Centre in Shaddongate closed and the Viceroy Indian Restaurant in Rigg Street expected to be closed for up to six months.

The River Caldew flooded at Lower Damside where the railway runs along the top of the arches and into the station. Businesses in the arches which were affected were: the Carlisle Golf Shop, J & L Motorcycles, Corkscrew Wines, Noise Hairdressers, Fred Bear Carpets, Margie's 'A Bit of a Do' cafe and the Superior Sewing Centre. On the

Lower Damside, photo. Marie Dickens

Shaddongate, photo. Martyn Boak.

other side of the road, the flood also affected Dobie's Vauxhall car showroom, the Harper & Hebson car showroom and the Indoor Bowling Alley.

It wasn't just businesses in Carlisle which were hit by the flooding and storms. In Cockermouth, Jennings Brewery flooded for the first time in living memory when the River Cocker burst its banks on Saturday. Managing director Mike Clayton said the floods had caused thousands of pounds of damage and brought

Shaddongate businesses were also flooded as was Wickes Home Improvement Centre, photos. Martyn Boak.

93

buildings and tore down gates and fences.

In Keswick, Booth's supermarket was flooded in the early hours of Saturday and the store had a power cut which resulted in freezer contents being destroyed and in Appleby businesses on The Sands, such as Bridge End Newsagents, Roy Ashley's Motors, the fish and chip shop, and the Co-op were counting the cost of the flood.

Junction Street, photo. Trevor Holloway.

brewing to a halt for a least two days. At the New Book Shop in Main Street around six inches of water got in through the front and back doors, despite the sand bags.

The storms affected the Sellafield nuclear power plant which lost its external electricity supply. Operations were disrupted until the plant's own generators kicked in. Sellafield also suffered damage from the gale force winds which ripped cladding off

Photo. David Jamison

Photo. Peter Longworth.

The media

One of the biggest problems during the storm was communication. With power lines down and sub-stations flooded the mobile phone network went down. Many land lines were also off because of flooded cables or lines brought down by fallen trees. With no power, people could not tune into the television or internet for news. The only means of communication left was word of mouth or radio, if you had the old-fashioned battery operated variety and tuned in to BBC Radio Cumbria which was running on an emergency generator with a skeleton staff. Milkmen, postmen and milk tanker drivers who got through despite fallen trees and floods became life lines, letting people know what was happening.

Ironically Carlisle's plight became world news and people all over the globe could see the situation but the city's residents were in a news blackout. People in Australia, for instance, could see the city's plight - polar traveller and environmentalist Robert Swan, who lives on Stainmore, was taking part in the Sydney to Hobart yacht race and telephoned friends in Cumbria after seeing Carlisle on the Australian news.

Cumbria's Chief Constable, Michael Baxter, said: 'The paradox was that we could not reach the people of Carlisle. The media all over the world knew what was happening but people in Carlisle knew nothing.'

Journalists from the national media were arriving in Carlisle by 11am to join dedicated local reporters and photographers covering the floods. There were journalists all over the city, including *Daily Mail* reporter Liz Hull who was posted to the city for two days to collect stories. *Sky News'* reporter Paul Harrison and cameraman Paul Shears had come up from Manchester and were sending pictures and reports around the world.

The *News & Star* sold a record 60,000 copies of its Monday special disaster paper which had to be printed in Barrow because of the power cuts in Carlisle. Keith Sutton, editorial director of Cumbrian Newspapers, said: 'When the Willowholme electricity supply went down it took 14 sub-stations with it. Our £5 million press shuddered to a halt just as we had started to run off copies of Saturday morning's *News & Star* with a stunning front-page picture of a submerged ambulance.

'Our private generator could only power our computers and internal lights, not the press. So no *News*

Sky News cameraman, Paul Shears,
photo. Peter Koronka.

95

Sending out the news by satellite, photo. Peter Koronka.

& *Star* appeared in Carlisle until 7.30am on Monday (that issue had been printed on our press at Barrow). The power cuts meant most people could not receive Radio Cumbria. TV transmitters were likewise knocked out. The police communicated physically by knocking on doors and later by delivering handbills. I raised the issue of the importance of our press for public information with the Chief Constable. Minutes later - on Sunday night - the power was turned on again by United Utilities. This enabled us to print more copies of Monday's *News & Star* Disaster Special in Carlisle. The public's thirst for information - and for pictures - was reflected in our incredible sales of Monday's paper - 60,000 and rising, almost double previous record sales in the paper's 46-year history. Wearing my hat as President of the Society of Editors, I am going to raise the issue of power generation, priorities in emergency and other issues such as mobile phone cut-offs, with the newly created Regional Media Emergency Forum (established in the wake of the recent terrorist threats).'

Cumbrian Newspapers offered free advertising to businesses affected by the flood so that they could keep in touch with their customers. The local papers were full of letters praising the emergency services and volunteers. There were also letters of support from people all over the country who know and love Carlisle. The *Cumberland News* planned to hold a civic reception to honour those who battled through atrocious conditions to help get people to safety during the floods. Those receiving the award were nominated by readers and were presented with a trophy by Carlisle's mayor, Ralph Aldersey.

BBC Radio Cumbria were praised for doing a brilliant job, working long hours with their studios powered by an emergency generator, keeping people informed and passing on messages from people who had no other way of keeping in touch with each other.

Mike Hutchinson-Brown said: 'We listened to BBC Radio Cumbria who've been fantastic in their role in communication with the city and the county. A strong and comforting presence in the silence...'

'The Reiver' wrote in the *News & Star*, 11 January, how brilliant the people at BBC Radio Cumbria had been over the weekend including Martin Plenderleith, Richard Nankivell, Gordon Swindlehurst, Mark McAlindon and Hannah

Morrison. He wrote: 'Normally, the dog-eat-dog world of regional journalism means that no newspaper would praise a rival media organisation. When confronted with anyone from Radio Cumbria or Border TV, my instinctive reaction is to make a sign of the cross and flee. But this time I feel I must make an exception - Radio Cumbria, you were fantastic.

'This was public-service broadcasting of the highest quality - up-to-the minute news provided with seamless efficiency and the utmost professionalism under great pressure.

'Despite the extreme circumstances, the reporters at Ground Zero managed to retain their sense of humour while back in the studio the peerless Plenderleith battled through eight hours on air on Saturday with a virtuoso performance.

'As the public and emergency services realised that they could communicate with each other via Radio Cumbria, the Carlisle studio virtually took on the role of a flood command centre.'

Steve Urquhart and Martin Plenderleith. were on duty at BBC Radio Cumbria for most of Saturday. Steve said: 'It all started for me when my kitchen window was leaking on Friday night and that was really annoying me. That's when I began to realise how dreadful the rain was. It was the end of the week and I was tired and looking forward to a lie in on Saturday morning. I went to bed at 1.50am, after falling asleep in front of the TV. I went into the bathroom and put the radio on and Radio Cumbria was still broadcasting and they shouldn't have been at that time in the morning. So I thought, 'OK this is getting worse.' Paul Braithwaite was on and he talked about the water having reached Brunton Park and Greystone Road where I live. I was getting quite scared so I rang into work and then thought perhaps

I should go in. I eventually got to work at about 5.30am on Saturday. One or two others were in and thankfully Martin made it. When we got there we realised that other staff were not going to make it because Carlisle was effectively cut off so we realised that we might be here for a while. Martin went on air at 6am to tell people the unfolding story and he had regular updates from the Environment Agency and spoke to some of our reporters who gave eye witness accounts. He also had reports from listeners, not only from Carlisle, but around the county.

'Barbara Butterworth from Bolton, near Appleby, came on air at about 6.45am and sounded in such despair. Martin continued on air through most of the morning. I went into the studio at 11am and normally I like to think we are quite prepared. But on this occasion I went into the studio and I had no idea what was going to happen or who we were going to talk to. What made it even stranger was that we knew by the amount of calls coming in that we had a lot of people listening and for a lot of people we were the only source of information. That made it even more bizarre really because you know that people are hanging on every word you say. On this occasion we really got that impression - that was what was so strange, and not having any sleep or any preparation. Between Martin and myself, we were on air for twelve hours.

'By 6pm Richard Corrie from Grinsdale had managed to get to the studio after wading through a lot of water - it took him hours. Another thing is that the power went off at 9.45am on Saturday morning and the emergency generator kicked in. We didn't get power back until 8pm on Sunday. Having no electricity limits the amount of things you can do as we only had power for one studio and ten computers.

We had staff over from other BBC stations, plus the website team and people were queuing up to use the computers.

'One of the more amusing stories was that we could not use the kettle. The chief engineer, Tim Tierney, told us: 'While the power's off, don't boil the kettle - it uses 20 per cent of our power so no cups of tea.' So we didn't have a drink until the Salvation Army brought us some tea which was much appreciated.

'That broadcast was the most difficult I have ever had to do and I've been broadcasting for twelve years because of sheer tiredness and the amount of calls, texts and e-mails that were coming in. I do want to say that our listeners have been extremely supportive. We had so many messages just to thank us for being on air at the weekend. People have sent boxes of chocolates and bottles of wine but our job is nothing compared to those of the emergency services.

' You are left with the sense that you did something good and that perhaps it's reminded us all of how important radio is. Hopefully after this people won't throw out their old battery radios - you never know when you might need them!'

Only two or three other members of staff were able to get to the studios, including news editor, Tom Speight, technical assistant, John McIntosh, Sue Cook and Steven Greaves who worked none stop through the night, answering telephone calls and Adam Flett who kept the BBC Cumbria website up-to-date with reports and photographs. The website received 3 million hits in 3 days which broke all records for BBC local websites across the country. Almost all members of Radio Cumbria's staff were personally affected. All the time Martin Plenderleith was broadcasting he was also worrying about his parents, Ian and Maureen, who live in Victoria Road, an area which he knew was flooded. Reporter Belinda Artingstoll's home was also badly flooded.

Martin manned a crisis special for 12 hours providing the only instant information available to local people. He said: 'I was due to do the breakfast show anyway. I live in the foothills of the Pennines and left home at around 4am on Saturday. I had to come through Haydon Bridge where they were already bailing people out. I hit a wall of water on the road and could see a helicopter above me. It was getting people out of cars and lorries which were stuck in the flood. I managed to get out and took some back roads to Carlisle, avoiding cars which were stuck. At 5.15am Hardwicke Circus was still dry but the water was rising. I went on air at 6am taking over from Paul Braithwaite and Sue Cook who had been answering telephone calls all night. Steve and I then ploughed through for twelve hours.'

The emergency generator could not supply full power so many of the technical aids to broadcasting were not available. Scribbled notes were passed to Martin who had to go back to basics and talked until his throat was dry, offering reassurance, advice and a link with the outside world.

He said: 'The other element is that my mum and dad live in one of the areas worst hit by the flooding. I managed to have a brief word with them in the morning before mobile phones stopped working and then lost contact with them. At 3.30 to 4pm the flood was at its peak and that night I stayed at Steve's house - he had narrowly missed being flooded. On Sunday morning someone got word to the police who found my parents and let me know that they were OK. My sister lives in County Durham and she was listening to the radio on the internet and I was able to let her know, on the radio, that they were OK.

'They are toughing it out at the moment but they will have to leave the house at some point. I got to see them on Sunday late evening - the flood had died back by then - to find my mum trying to cook a bacon sandwich upstairs.

'This has connected me to a story like I have never been connected before. Saturday and Sunday was just completely ad hoc. We were trying to get as many people on air as possible and we were relying on the community itself to be our reporters. All we have done is to act as a vehicle for people to tell their own stories. It has continued to unfold from there. We were always a consumer based programme and now it's just how to survive the floods and pestilence, not just for the Carlisle area but for the rest of the county too. A week after the floods we were still getting people ringing in to tell their story.

'This morning when I was in town the owner of a café promised me free coffee for life because she had been stranded without power and thought

Steve Urquhart and Martin Plenderleith, BBC Radio Cumbria, photo. Peter Koronka.

Radio Cumbria was a life line and I have had lots of cards from people all over.'

At the end of the week of the flood BBC Radio Cumbria broadcast a special half-hour programme called *Dark Water Rising*. It brought together the best of the station's broadcasts about the flood and was produced by Gordon Swindlehurst who was the first reporter on the scene in Appleby as the river burst its banks.

Hardwicke Circus with the Sands Centre in the distance, photo. Peter Longworth.

Schools

Ninety per cent of Cumbria's schools were closed on the Monday following the storm as they were affected by flooding, structural damage to buildings and power cuts. Sadly some schools were so badly damaged by flooding that they faced weeks, if not months, of closure.

In Carlisle students who were due to sit AS and GCSE exams were allowed to go in to sit the exams, but the circumstances were very difficult. Students were unable to revise because of flooded homes, lack of sleep and sodden books. Even if their homes hadn't been flooded there were power cuts which meant students were not able to have hot meals or to use computers for two days before the exams. Those who did manage to sit exams would be given special dispensation by examiners. Students who were not able to take their exams because they could not get in to their schools had another opportunity to sit the exams later in the year. Some students, like Mercedes Boyd chose not to do the exams because she was volunteering to help people in a reception centre at her school. Both the North Cumbria

Newman School, photo. Jeff Gibson.

Photo. Jeff Gibson.

Technology College and Norman Street School, were used as emergency reception centres.

Radio Cumbria were able to let anxious parents and children know which schools were open and closed across the county.

Three of Carlisle's secondary schools were extensively damaged by the floods and were left facing repair bills which ran into millions.

Head of St Aidan's County High School, Martin Murphy said his school building would need around £1 million in repairs. He said there was a lot of damage to the ground floor and sports area and it had caused, 'a great deal of sadness.' The school had

forty dehumidifiers working to try to dry out sodden classrooms. Contractors and structural engineers were in the school helping with clearing up the mess.

One of the worst affected schools was Newman School which was expected to be closed for several months. The impressive computer suite and the new dining area were ruined by around four feet of water.

The following story was in the *Cumberland News*, 14 January 2005: Newman School and St Aidan's were especially badly hit by the floods. Students who were taking their national AS exams were able to do the exams at North Cumbria Technology College. Newman's ground floor, including its new computer suite and dining room has been ruined. Deputy head, Peter Naylor, said the ground floor was 'a total loss.' He said the school wanted to thank the North Cumbria Technology College for their support and co-operation and they were working to find alternative teaching locations so that students could go back to school at least part-time.

Trinity School was not quite so badly damaged but still needed a major clean-up. The boiler rooms were flooded with muddy water which meant the heating system wasn't working and the school was also without power.

Head Alan Mottershead said: 'The eastern end and the main sports arena, the Eden dining room and kitchen were flooded and will be out of action for some time. But we count ourselves extremely lucky when you look at other schools.'

Crosby-on-Eden school had a new floor in the school hall, especially for gym lessons, and this was ruined by the floods. The school has 84 pupils - their work - drawings, writing, text books - lay sodden and ruined amongst the mud and slime. Head Mary Alston told the *Cumberland News*: 'The water got into all the lockers and the children's work is

The interior of Newman School,
photo. Cumbrian Newspapers Ltd.

A bullock which was washed away by the floods had an amazing excape and ended up in the playground of St. Aidan's School, which is also pictured below, photos. Peter Cockshott, from a mobile phone.

destroyed. We will repair the school but much of the work is lost forever.'

St Martin's College was not flooded but was closed for two days because of lack of power, access problems and the telephone system being out of operation. A spokesman said all the students in the campus's halls of residence had escaped the floods uninjured.

Farms

Farms and livestock were badly affected by the flooding. Cattle, sheep and horses were moved from low-lying land near rivers on Friday as rivers began to break their banks and the torrential rain continued. Many animals were saved in heroic rescue bids but sadly some were swept away. The floods left thousands of acres of land under water, damaging crops.

A dead cow was seen floating along Etterby Terrace and a bullock, washed down river by the floods, ended up, still alive, in St. Aidan's School playground. Thirty sheep drowned in the River Tweed near Berwick when an island they were standing on became inundated with water. Some farmers said that the damage caused by the floods and storms were worse than foot and mouth disease, four years earlier.

Power cuts added to the difficulties and farmers with new born lambs which had to be kept warm were using oil heaters and others were using generators so they could milk cows. Many farmers were out with their chainsaws the day after the storm, clearing fallen trees from the roads. Their efforts

Flooded farmland near Penrith, photo. Peter Koronka.

came in for praise from members of the public.

NFU representative, Mike Sanderson, from Appleby said: 'It's been absolutely unprecedented. Even the old farmers are not saying, 'It was much worse in such and such a year.''

Lindsay Tuck from Moorhouse Mill, near Wigton, on the Solway flood plain managed to rescue her flock of sheep despite deep flood water and strong currents when the River Wampool broke its banks. She said: 'I have a small flock of pedigree Jacob sheep. We often have a little flood but at 4pm the water was rising very rapidly in the field. In another half an hour the water had risen a foot and by this time it was getting dark. Some of the sheep are in lamb and some are last year's lambs. I was on my own with my son and the window cleaner, Harry Coulthard, turned up and he helped. One of our neighbours, Alan Pattinson, who is 76-years-old was marvellous and came and put straw in the buildings for us.

'My husband, Tony, had just gone back to work after recovering from a fractured femur. He got home and was helping too. By 7pm the water was very high and I'd been in the water for two hours getting the young sheep out. We just had the big ones to rescue and they were absolutely petrified. Tony and I got back into the field and the water was thigh deep and we managed to get to the sheep in the worst field. They were so frightened and were up to their noses in water. We managed to get the lead sheep and make her swim and then they all swam in a line and we got them to safety.

'In the meantime my 21-year-old daughter, Gemma, had had a car accident. She was OK but her car was damaged so it was taken to Willowholme and, of course, it was flooded with all her things inside.

'Harry, the window cleaner, was absolutely wonderful. He stayed here for three hours. He doesn't know anything about sheep but he helped enormously. At first we tried to lift the sheep over the fence but they were too heavy because they were water-logged. I really thought I was going to lose my sheep. Our neighbour did have eighteen sheep that were drowned.'

Retired farmer Joseph Watson of Crosby-on-Eden remembers the flood of 1968 after which he built a bank around his property and installed a generator. He also had a level marked on his house to show where the water came to in 1968 and this time fortunately, his home was not flooded, though other properties in the village were badly affected.

At Orton the Farmers' Market was postponed despite its hope to be open whatever the weather. Organiser Jane Brook said stallholders were unable to get to Orton because they were dealing with floods. Those who did try to get through found the roads blocked by fallen trees and overturned lorries. In addition the village had no electricity. It was the first time the market had had to be cancelled since the foot and mouth epidemic in 2001.

The following story is from the *Cumberland News*: At Neil Fell's Scotby farm only 30 acres of his 650 acre farm escaped the flood waters. Wheelbarrow Hall Farm has had many floods but this flood exceeded all expectations. In four generations at the farm, it was the first time since 1947 that the family have lost cattle to the flood water.

Neil said: 'We live with the risk of the river every day, but that Saturday was an exceptional day.' He knew the river was going to flood and had moved cattle to higher ground earlier that day, including 20 young cattle to a field behind Tesco's that hasn't flooded in living memory. The flood washed all 20 away but amazingly most survived. Three were washed up alive down stream at Stoney Holme Golf Course. Two were found in Rickerby Park and eight made it across the river where they were marooned on an island. A couple didn't make it and were found at Rickerby Park and near the Edenside cricket club. Neil said: 'We haven't given up hope that the rest might have survived.'

At nearby Warwick Holme farm the fifty-year-old flood defences were breached in seven places and a deluge hit the farm. More than 300 sheep which were wintering at the farm, were lost and ten cattle were drowned in their stalls when the water rose to six feet. Steven Peel, farm manager for Holme Gate Farms which includes Warwick Holme Farm, helped to rescue three families living on the estate and then returned to try to save the livestock. As Steven and his wife Mary were moving a flock of sheep to safety a section of the flood defences gave way and the water shot through with huge force but they did manage to save these sheep.

When the flood water receded animal carcasses were found trapped in trees or caught in hedges. The farm has also lost thousands of pounds worth of crops. Steven said: 'It will take us years to recover

Flooded farmland near Carlisle, photo. Peter Koronka.

from this. It could be worse than foot and mouth.'

Peter Vasey and his son Giles, who farm at Warwick Bridge, faced a race against time to rescue their herd of pedigree Charolais cattle from the rising flood water. Wading through water at least four feet deep, and rising by the minute, Peter, his family and some helpers tried to open the sheds to let the animals out. Fifty terrified cows and calves were evacuated through the torrent and led to higher ground and 20 bulls were moved to safer buildings. Only one, a calf just one day old, was washed away by the raging water and was quickly captured after one of the eight strong team of rescuers grabbed its head. They formed a human chain against the current until it could be lifted to the safety of a nearby vehicle. Peter raised the alarm early on Saturday morning when he realised the river, which is only 300 yards from Holme House farm, had risen dramatically. Fearing for his livestock he tried to block the flow of water into the sheds but there was no stopping it. At 4.30am Peter called for reinforcements and his son Giles and two friends came to help evacuate the animals. Four retained firefighters from Longtown also came to their aid.

Peter said: 'It looked impossible. We were wading through a torrent of water and the current was so strong, you struggled to get your footing. We didn't know if the animals would be washed away, but if we had left them, they would have been drowned. The animals were terrified and didn't want to move. It took a huge effort to get them out of the building. The water was up to the calves' necks.'

After evacuating the cows and calves the men went back to rescue the bulls which had become very distressed as the water rose. They were moved to another shed but were still standing in three and a half feet of water. Peter said: 'It wasn't ideal, but at least they were safe. They were there for about twelve hours until we could move them again. We were extremely lucky. If we'd waited another ten minutes, we would have lost a considerable amount of stock. I still don't know how we achieved it. You don't consider the implications of what you're doing at the time. You just want to get the livestock to safety.'

The floods in Peter, and his wife Vanessa's, home were chest deep. Peter said: 'We did as much as we could in the house by moving things upstairs, but the cattle had to take priority. A helicopter arrived to air-lift us away, but we didn't want to leave the stock.' Friends and neighbours rallied around afterwards to help clean up the mess - a three foot deep layer of straw, silt and manure, all mixed together.

Peter said: 'We were anticipating the river would rise but nothing like this. We've lived here for 40 years and never seen anything like it. It's a disaster area at the moment, but we survived foot and mouth, and we'll survive this.'

Services

Power lines were damaged by trees and electricity sub-stations were flooded leaving 170,000 homes without power by midnight on Saturday and some people facing days, weeks or even months without an electricity supply. In total more than 250,000 homes and businesses in Cumbria were affected by the power failures.

The familiar orange glow of Carlisle's street lights was gone, traffic lights weren't working, shops and homes were in complete darkness. The streets were silent as no traffic could get through and there were no people talking or shouting as they came out of pubs and clubs. The only sound across the city was that of lapping water and the noise of alarms going off, triggered by the power cuts.

Charlie Cornish, managing director of United Utilities North West said: 'The region has experienced the worst storms in decades, with winds up to 100 miles per hour and severe flooding in some areas. This has had an unprecedented impact on the electricity network and has resulted in a huge number of faults for us to repair in very difficult conditions.

'Our main priority has been to fix these faults as quickly as possible in order to get customers' electricity supply restored. More than 250,000 homes and businesses in Cumbria were affected by power failures... We have had over 800 people working around the clock to restore power to our customers and to repair the severe damage that the storms have caused to our electricity network.'

United Utilities has an electricity bulk supply point at Willowholme which was flooded under three feet of water on Saturday. The company said that in total fourteen sub-stations in Carlisle were fully or partly submerged.

Consumers criticised the United Utilities' information service which was a recorded message, leaving no opportunity to speak to anyone. The company said their call centres had received as many calls in a

One of the United Utilities engineers working in Warwick Road, photo. Peter Koronka.

Greystone Road, photo. Peter Koronka.

day as they would normally expect in a month and were unable to cope. Later United Utilities set up a mobile customer centre in Carlisle to help people affected by the floods and the power failures.

United Utilities' workmen came in for a lot of praise for the work they did to restore power to stricken regions. The company brought in around 450 engineers from Scotland and the south of England to help get the situation back to normal. The damage to the power infrastructure caused by the storm was expected to cost more than £1 million to repair.

Mr. Clarkson was one of those on site for the duration. He said: 'We've got gangs of lads going round the properties now but restoring power really depends on the state of the inside of the houses.' Electricity and water make a lethal combination and until buildings are dried out it was unsafe to switch on the power. Around 600 homes were expected to be without electricity for longer periods because of flood damage. Plaster absorbed the flood water and in many cases the plaster had to be removed and the houses renovated before power could be restored. It

was thought that some families would not be able to return to their homes for six to nine months.

Following the floods, United Utilities announced it planned to spend half a million pounds on building flood defences for its £2 million Willowholme installation. The bulk supply point supplies six sub-stations across the city. The flood water tripped all 24 circuit breakers cutting power to 50,000 homes in the city. Workmen couldn't get near to start repair works until Sunday afternoon because the water was so high. The Willowholme sub-station was later pumped out by firefighters using heavy-duty pumps. The situation was made worse because power lines in other parts of the county had been brought down by the gales. A spokesman said the Willowholme site had never been flooded before but there were now plans for a concrete bank with built in pumps to protect the installation.

United Utilities worked all week to re-connect electricity supplies across the county and the final twenty households were re-connected on 17 January, more than a week after the storm.

The company agreed to pay compensation to thousands of people who lost their electricity, including 1,000 households in Carlisle. The company is obliged to pay out if customers are without power for more than 48 hours.

BT engineers were working to try to get city phones back on line. A spokesman said: 'The amount of water we had here was way above the pressure the

cables are designed for. The cables got very wet and stopped working. We are working around the clock trying to get the phones back on.' Engineers were working all weekend but because of the severe conditions there was a shortage of vans with the right equipment. Later in the week though people and equipment were being brought in from other areas. Phone lines were affected by the high winds and fallen trees. Mobile phone networks were also down as there was no electricity to power the signal towers.

Carlisle Magistrates' Court in Rickergate was hit by power and heating problems caused by the floods. All custody and urgent cases were dealt with at Penrith magistrates court or in a courtroom at the Crown Court building.

The Royal Mail cancelled all deliveries in Carlisle during the floods and some libraries were closed because of the power cuts.

Photos. Peter Koronka.

Sport and Recreation

Carlisle United's ground at Brunton Park just off Warwick Road was under eight feet of water - an estimated 20 million litres which turned the pitch into a lake - and there were fears that the stadium had been structurally damaged by the force of the water.

The ground floor of the stadium was devastated by the filthy water. Changing rooms, bars, offices, boardroom, toilets, the gym, treatment room, kitchens, the club shop and many players' cars were all swamped.

United had been due to play at home to Redditch in the FA Trophy on the Saturday of the flood but had to call off all scheduled home fixtures. The team had to play a home game at Workington Reds' Borough Park for the first time in more than 20 years. The last time they had to borrow their old enemy's ground was when their pitch was frozen solid in January 1982.

Club owner Fred Story said the goal posts were completely submerged at the Water Works end of the pitch. The club was being run from his company's offices at Story Construction on the Burgh Road industrial estate and workers from his firm were helping with the clear up operation.

Carlisle United Football Club, photo. Cumbrian Newspapers Ltd.

Photo. Peter Koronka.

The clean up was a huge task and it was expected to take up to a month. Luckily engineers had confirmed that the stadium had escaped structural damage. United were overwhelmed by the number of volunteers who helped to clean up the stadium.

Carlisle United player-boss Paul Simpson described the week of the flood as 'the most traumatic' of his life in an interview with the *Cumberland News*. He had taken off his football training kit and put on wellies and protective gloves to help with the clean up at Brunton Park. Simpson said: 'After the Crawley game I was raging at the way we had performed in the second half. We dropped three points and I was very disappointed.

'Then you come home and see all that has happened and football fades into the background. The last two or three days have been about beginning to clear up and football has not really been on the minds of anyone.

'Going down Warwick Road brings a lump to your throat and at the end of the day, although the football club has suffered, everything is covered by insurance so we haven't got much to moan about really.'

On Friday, almost a week after the flood, two

113

Photos. Peter Koronka.

goldfish were found in a puddle on the Carlisle United ground. The club put out an appeal in the local media to find the owners. It was a *Finding Nemo* moment and was at least something to smile at after the misery of the week. Maggie Alston, a resident of Brunton Crescent, also found a fish in her garden which was still

Bitts Park, photo. Kenny Turner.

alive. She took it in a dog bowl to ask a neighbour in Greystone Road who has a fishpond if it belonged to him. He said he had lost twelve fish in total.

Next door to the football club, Carlisle' Rugby Football Club suffered similar devastation when it was under nearly six feet of water. The changing rooms and clubhouse were ruined, along with some of the club's machinery. The clear up here was expected to take up to four months.

Carlisle Squash Club, next door to the rugby club on Warwick Road, was also awash. The place was said to be in ruins with the floor buckled and everything on the ground floor damaged.

Carlisle Cricket Club was seriously damaged by the floods and the clean up was expected to last months. The new £7,000 electronic scoreboard at the club was ruined when it was submerged in water. Inside the pavilion was devastated with water three quarters of the way to the ceiling. The dance floor was lifted up and a tank for heating fuel floated away.

Bitts Park, photo. Peter Koronka.

The Stony Holme Golf Club was closed and two men had to be airlifted from the clubhouse when they were cut off by fast rising water. The restaurant and bar areas had seen most damage. Eden Golf Club in Crosby-on-Eden was inundated with flood water over a foot deep which damaged some machinery.

The Sheepmount athletics station was undergoing a £3.6 million renovation but much of the work was destroyed by the flood. The stadium has around 50 acres of land some of which was under fifteen feet of water. A new floor which had just been put down was damaged as were the old changing rooms.

Chatsworth Tennis Club had two indoor courts damaged by the flooding. The acrylic-style flooring was covered in three feet of water. There was also damage to the clubhouse.

Bitts Park was badly flooded and two days later was still partially covered in water. It was dotted with debris left by the floods - a rabbit hutch, wheely bins, logs, a child's umbrella, a hot water bottle, Christmas cards and all manner of sundry items. Rickerby Park was also flooded.

Upper Eden Rugby Club's match was cancelled because of the weather so members of the team went to the aid of Gary Alderson who owns Alderson's Garage, Nateby, near Kirkby Stephen. Part of the roof of his garage had been torn off by the high winds and deposited in a nearby field. Gary's sons, Simon and Paul, both play for the club and, along with Karl Haygarth, Ian Gowing, Duncan Rose, Colin Wolstenholme and Colin Sowerby, they helped put a temporary roof on the building. It took them five hours to patch up the damaged roof and make it safe. Mr Alderson said: 'It was one of the wildest nights we have had up here for a long time. I would like to thank the rugby lads for their help. They brought with them a real team spirit.' By evening the garage was almost watertight.

There was 61 inches of water on Appleby Bowling Club's green where there is a mark showing the flood

Bitts Park, photo, Jeff Gibson.

Bitts Park Gardens taken from the subway entrance, photo, Steve Weatherill and Ann Butler.

peak in 1968 of 59.5 inches. The pavilion was damaged by the filthy water and one member said it was a 'disaster'.

Appleby Cricket Club's pavilion was badly affected by two feet of flood water. The flood left a trail of sludge, damaged electrical fittings and ruined carpets. It also washed away beer barrels, destroyed fences and washed away wicket covers.

Transport

Roads, railways and bridges were severely affected by the storm and floods. Carlisle was virtually cut off from the outside world with all routes into the city impassable, except for Scotland Road. The city's main road junction at Hardwicke Circus, was transformed into a lake with traffic lights poking out surreally from the waves.

At the height of the flooding not a single train was running in Cumbria because of landslides, fallen trees and floods on the tracks. Carlisle's bus service was crippled when the bus depot was flooded and across the county lorries and trees were blown over blocking roads and many routes were affected by flooding or fallen power lines.

In Carlisle roads which flooded included Castle Way, Caldewgate, Shaddongate, Warwick Road and London Road. Warwick Road remained closed to traffic for three days while the massive job of clearing up went on.

Traffic lights were not working across most of the city because of floods and power cuts. Car parks were free as none of the ticket machines were working and traffic wardens were off duty for four days

Castle Way to Hardwicke Circus, photo, Kenny Turner.

Hardwicke Circus, photo, Martyn Boak.

Underpass, Castle Way,
photo, Jeff Gibson.

Above, flooded underpass under Castle Way from West Tower Street and right, flooded car park, Rickergate, photos, Peter Longworth.

The old road bridge over the River Petteril, near Newbiggin Hall, just outside Carlisle, was damaged by the flood water. Half of the central pier was ripped away leaving a huge hole in the road above, photos, Peter Koronka

after the floods. As the flood water began to recede, London Road became the main route in and out of Carlisle. At one point the garage on London Road was the only one able to sell fuel as other garages in the city were hit by flooding or power cuts.

The southbound M6 was closed for a time as were the A66, A69 and A591. There was a spate of accidents on the M6 in the ferocious weather and eight lorries were blown over on Shap Fell. The A66 was closed to high-sided vehicles for more than a week but, despite the closure, some lorries tried to cross the fells and were blown over on the dual carriageway at Stainmore. On Saturday on the A1 25 lorries were blown over near Darlington, leaving the road closed in both directions. The A69, Carlisle to Hexham road, was closed for two days at Warwick Bridge because of the flooding.

The cost of repairing flood damaged roads was expected to rise in the weeks and months following the storm as weakened roads were discovered. The foundations of a section of the A66 near Appleby

The road to Little Corby at Warwick Bridge, photo. Anton Hodge.

were damaged by flooding which caused subsidence and had to be repaired immediately. There were fears that, as well as structural problems to the roads, some road drainage systems had also been damaged and that many bridges would need significant repair work.

In the last great flood of 1968 the old stone Langwathby Bridge was washed away. The Army built a temporary replacement metal bridge, known as the Bailey Bridge, over the River Eden. The bridge features in the *Guinness Book of Records* as the oldest temporary bridge in the country. Almost forty years after it was built, the temporary bridge survived this even greater flood, which was more than three feet higher than that of 1968 and produced much more damage. Villagers were forced to make long detours during and after the floods. County council surveyors confirmed that the bridge itself had not been damaged. However, the force of the flood had washed away a large section of the A686 Penrith to Alston road near the bridge, leaving the road closed for four days. Repair work was expected to cost more than £60,000.

Above Caldew Maltings and below, the Viaduct, photos, Jeff Gibson.

Left, the Lower Viaduct area and below, the main London to Glasgow railway line at Caldew Bridge, photos. Kenny Turner.

Looking across the railway towards Shaddongate, photo. Jeff Gibson.

In Carlisle, Stagecoach North West's Willowholme depot was submerged causing damage estimated at £3 million to 70 buses, some of which were so badly damaged they couldn't be restored. The company had to borrow 50 vehicles from other cities across the country in order to keep their timetable running. Managing director of Stagecoach North West, Nigel Barrett, told the *Cumberland News:* 'We had a flood warning on Friday but that usually means a couple of inches of water in the depot. Nothing prepared us for what was to come. The depot was dry as a bone when we locked up at 2am but by 3.30am it was under water. There was no time to get the buses out.'

The main London to Glasgow railway line was closed at Carlisle because of serious flooding which in places washed away the ground supporting the track. Passengers on Virgin Trains which use the route had to transfer to coaches for the journey between Carlisle and Lockerbie. The line was finally fully open again more than a week later.

Two landslides hit Cumbrian railways but no passengers were affected as luckily both lines had been shut for weekend maintenance. The main west

Photograph above, taken from Caldew Bridge and below showing Viaduct Estate Road and the main West Coast Railway, photos. Peter Longworth.

Above, this is the damage left by flood water in a brand new car. It was obvious which cars had been flooded as the head lights still had brown water inside them and the cars themselves were full of condensation.

Left, cars and vans floated away in the flood - this van was left wedged between a tree and a wall on Warwick Road, photos. Peter Koronka.

Loading and removing flood damaged cars on Warwick Road, photos. Peter Koronka.

It was easy to spot flood damaged cars - they were dripping with condensation. The owner of this car had left a note for the traffic wardens as the car was in a public car park, photo. Peter Koronka.

Agency and Cumbria Fire and Rescue Service worked to recover the tank before its contents polluted the lake - around 30 gallons of diesel was spilled but it could have been much worse.

coast line was affected by a landslide near to Shap Wells Hotel where a section of the bank had been washed away. On the Settle-Carlisle railway line there was another landslide a few miles south of Kirkby Stephen.

A total of 74 boats across the area slipped their moorings and were washed away. Three launches belonging to the Keswick Launch Company came loose from their moorings at the height of the storm and were adrift on Derwentwater. The *Lady Derwentwater*, a wooden launch, was the most seriously damaged - she was blown on to Derwent Island. A diesel tank from the company's landings was also swept away and left floating on Derwentwater. Staff from the Environment

Devonshire Walk car park, photo. Peter Longworth.

Local authorities

Carlisle City Council was left with a huge clean up operation, not just in the city, but also in the Civic Centre which stood in eight feet of water. The building was still partially under water on Sunday and on Monday teams started to pump the water out of the basement. Carlisle City Council Building Surveyor Mark Irwin said: 'We are busy trying to get pumped out. The basement is under the whole building and houses the plant and boiler rooms.'

Mr Irwin said he thought it could be six months before the building was fully open though the council hoped to have a skeleton staff in soon. Other council staff moved up to Boustead's Grassings where they were accommodated in temporary offices in Portakabins.

The filthy flood water left the civic centre dangerous with thick, slippery mud and debris all over the floor. The customer service centre downstairs had been newly decorated with new furniture and computers. The photographs in this chapter show the mud-covered customer centre, piles

Carlisle Civic Centre,
photo. Kenny Turner.

The Civic Centre and Carlisle Police Station,
photo. Jeff Gibson.

of water-logged computers and ruined furniture which had to be thrown away.

Meanwhile the council had a duty to help residents coping with the floods - they had to clean streets, remove rubbish and offer health and other advice to residents.

Council officials set up an emergency service to help with the clear up. There were 300 council work- ers helping to clean the city's streets, removing debris left by the flood and power-washing some streets to remove the mud, as well as removing flood damaged property from houses which was piled on the streets.

The council also had to warn people about the pub- lic health aspects of the flood, reminding them to wear plastic gloves and to wash their hands regular- ly if they were handling flood damaged items as the water could carry bacteria. The city council set up an information point for residents in Tullie House while the civic centre was out of action.

Cumbria County Council was under pressure to cope with the extraordinary emergency. Highways teams worked all hours to clear fallen trees, restore street lighting, move debris and repair damage to bridges and roads. Many roads were closed because of flooding and people were being advised to take extreme care on the roads and not to use foot bridges until the council had time to check them. An emergency phone line was set up to deal with enquiries about flooding.

The county council's emergency planning officer Donald Norrie was on duty while events unfolded.

Above Carlisle Civic Centre, photo. David Jamison.

Left, floods near the civic centre, photo. Peter Longworth.

The council was aware of the severe weather warning from the Meteorological Office and the Environment Agency. Mr Norrie decided to open schools as emergency reception centres and he established a disaster control centre at Carlisle Castle. Mr Norrie said in an interview with the *Cumberland News*: 'The widespread nature and incredible severity and rapidity of this problem was quite daunting and not at all foreseeable. Meteorologists told us of depressions coming in, which looked fairly average until they got close to the British Isles. Then they wound up and we got two months' rainfall in the space of 24 hours.'

In the aftermath of the floods the county council consulted with the authorities which dealt with the floods in Boscastle, Cornwall. The council was focusing on six areas affected by the flooding - community and welfare, infrastructure, public buildings, schools, businesses and finding the resources to pay for work needed. Cumbria County Council leader, Tim Stoddard, appealed for

Inside Carlisle City Council's Civic Centre the newly refurbished reception centre is ruined, photo. Peter Koronka.

Above a pile of computers, newly installed into the civic centre but ruined by the flood. Right, some of the ruined items from the civic centre, photos. Peter Koronka.

the Government to make extra emergency funding available and for the Prime Minister, Tony Blair, to visit the area so he could see for himself the devastation caused by the storm.

District councils across the county struggled to deal with the exceptionally severe weather. Eden District Council issued more than 3,000 sandbags and, at Appleby, a contractor was asked to sandbag the Sands area of the town. Despite the precautions the area suffered flooding. Sandbags were distributed in Eamont

Right, a council street sweeper tackling the mud on Warwick Road and below, pumping out the basement of the civic centre, photos. Peter Koronka.

Bridge and the council helped residents in Carlisle by sending 1,000 sandbags and a team of workmen to sandbag flood hit parts of the city. The district council said that residents and businesses hit by the floods could be exempt from paying council tax and business rates for up to a year.

In South Lakeland around one third of council houses had suffered some form of damage and the picture was similar West Cumbria.

The hurricane

One of the most devastating aspects of the storm was the wind. It was hurricane force by late on Friday night and reached its peak early on Saturday morning. Wind speeds ranged from 55mph to gusts of 128mph which was recorded at the summit of Great Dun Fell. A similar wind speed was recorded on Shap Fell and, no doubt, the wind speed was similar on all the fell tops. In the Eden Valley a wind speed of 89mph was recorded at Warcop, near Appleby.

Sadly, cabinet maker, Michael Scott, 63, was killed in his caravan at Halls Hill Farm, Hethersgill, when the wall of a barn was blown on to his home. A man from Long Marton, near Appleby, had a very lucky escape when a tree landed on his car.

The west of the county bore the brunt of the hurricane force. Many homes in Whitehaven lost roofs, garages, fences and greenhouses. A wind speed of 120mph was recorded at Workington Port which

Photos. Jeff Gibson.

137

sustained thousands of pounds of damage with many roofs torn off buildings. More than 400 buildings in Workington were partially or completely stripped of slates. Every street was littered with slates and many cars were damaged. Chimneys were blown over and windows smashed by flying debris.

In Maryport boats were blown over and part of the roof of Maryport Infants School was torn off. Council workers were working round the clock to move fallen trees and debris left by the storm. The roof was ripped off Frizington Co-op and torrential rain poured into the building during the height of the storm.

In Carlisle the winds brought down a huge beech tree near the old St. Joseph's Residential Home. David Lindsay and Billy Robb, both from Carlisle, were working on clearing fallen trees for Go4Skills who were contracted by Carlisle City Council. Photo. Peter Koronka.

St John's Church, Keswick, was damaged in the high wind with lead capping peeled back, tiles loosened and a fallen ceiling in part of the church. Parishioners turned out to help clear up the mess so that the Sunday service could still be held.

It was estimated that half a million trees were

blown over on Forestry Commission land across the county and countless other trees on private land were uprooted. A spokesman for the commission said there had been 'significant' damage to Cumbria's forests. Commission workers were busy clearing fallen trees from car parks and paths in the Lake District following the storm.

Lake District National Park Authority workers also had weeks of work in front of them to clear up the destruction caused by the storm, including fallen trees and footpaths which had been washed away by floods.

The National Trust owns a lot of property in the Lake District and many trees were lost to the gales. Trust staff and foresters worked hard to clear away the debris from properties. At Sizergh Castle what was thought to be the tallest Austrian Pine in Cumbria was cut in half by the wind and at Fell Foot on Windermere the timber boat house disappeared under water and the trust's tea room and shop were flooded. In the Derwentwater area there were three landslips and

Retired farmer Mr John Alderson from Stainmore - the gable end of his home which was moved by the force of the hurricane, photo. Peter Koronka.

hundreds of trees blown over. At Aira Force waterfall there was extensive damage to the arboretum and at Langdale a campsite was flooded. Garth Wood, near Keswick, which is owned by the Woodland Trust, had to be closed until damaged trees could be moved.

Professional tree surgeons were kept employed across the county for weeks to help clear up the mess. Sadly a man from Wigton ended up in intensive care after a storm-damaged tree he was cutting up fell and crushed his legs.

Further inland, at Kirkby Stephen, the playgroup lost its shed in the storm and part of a roof was ripped off a building in Faraday Road. A large tree hit a house at Helbeck, near Brough, owned by the McAllister family. The tree also hit electricity cables but luckily no one was injured.

Even further to the east, Gateshead engineers were concerned about the affect the high winds had had on the Angel of the North. The monument is designed to stand winds in excess of 100mph.

A Stainmore couple were forced to move out of their home which was severely damaged in the storm. Incredibly, one end of the building has actually moved, a chimney was blown down and almost all the roof was damaged.

Retired farmer John Alderson and his wife Ann from Station House, thought their house was going to fall down at the height of the storm. Mr Alderson said: 'It was terrifying. The chimney came down at 2.30am and that woke us up. There was such a bang, I thought the house was coming down.

'Straightaway I looked out of the window and I then presumed it was the chimney. I got dressed and had a cup of tea and just sat. I did not dare go out. At 5am the roof slates were flying around and the

Mrs Ann Alderson, rescuing possessions from the damaged house, photo. Peter Koronka.

house just shook. It was terrifying. The house was just shaking and I thought any minute the house is going to fall. There were slates going everywhere. It was awful. The slates were flying around in the wind and if you'd gone outside you'd have been killed.

'It's now raining into every room of our house and we've had to move out. It's an absolute mess. It's been terrible. I've never known anything like it.

Part of the chimney went through the hall roof, photo. Peter Koronka.

'All the chimneys have moved and one has fallen through the house. Even the gable end of the house has moved. The surveyor has been in and he says one end of the house has moved because the walls are no longer straight. The insurance people and the surveyor say the house is too dangerous to live in at the moment.'

The force of the storm and flying slates broke many windows. One slate had embedded itself into a door and another had flown 100 feet and broken the wooden rail of a gate. The chimney had smashed through the hall roof and the ceiling below. Other ceilings in the house were damaged by the water coming in.

At first John and Ann stayed in the house, moving their bed down to the living room, but it was raining in everywhere. John said: 'We were catching water at the end of the bed and it's coming through every ceiling.'

Neighbours and friends have been incredible and have helped the couple to move furniture and precious items to a temporary home at Barras Farm, where they plan to stay until their house is repaired.

Ann said: 'We are not supposed to be in the house too much but we are just taking out what's essential. There's not an awful lot left and the roof is too far gone to put tarpaulins or anything on - it's too dangerous.'

John and Ann moved into the old station hotel which was built in the early 1860s, about twelve years ago. The house was completely renovated at that time and has been well maintained since with a builder visiting every year to carry out routine maintenance and to check the roof.

Inside John and Ann had the house snug and beautifully decorated. It was a very stressful experience to see all their hard work destroyed and to have to organise insurers, surveyors and builders.

Mr Alderson said: 'I have been ill with it. I haven't been sleeping at all, though last night, a week after the storm, I did sleep for about three hours. It's an old house and it's stood some terrific storms, but that was the highest wind I have ever known.'

Around the county

The storm which caused so much damage at Carlisle swept in off the Atlantic, hitting Ireland first where there were 90 mile an hour winds and many people were left without electricity. A lorry driver died when his vehicle was blown off the Foyle Bridge in Londonderry.

Across Cumbria, Scotland and the North East, the storm continued to bring death and destruction. It didn't stop there though. By Saturday night the storm was sweeping over northern Europe where it killed another ten people and left hundreds of thousands without power. In Sweden six people were killed, including two whose cars were struck by falling trees and four people were killed in Denmark. Meteorologists said it was the worst storm to hit Scandinavia in years.

In the UK two men were drowned in swollen rivers. One man was washed away by the River Aire at Apperley Bridge, near Bradford, on Saturday lunchtime. Police tried to reach the man but the conditions were too treacherous. Another man was drowned in a river in Scotland.

Carlisle was the epicentre of the floods in Cumbria

Flooding at Eamont Bridge, photo. Fred Wilson.

Floods at Warwick Bridge, where the A69 was under so much water it had to be closed, photos. Anton Hodge.

The River Eden in flood, photo. Fred Wilson.

but across the district the water reached record levels as it touched the top of bridge arches and flooded over into towns and villages. People were evacuated because of flooding in Keswick, Appleby, Kendal, Longtown, Cockermouth, Wigton, Kendal and Shap - in fact in almost every area of the county.

The Rivers Tyne and Wear were up to record levels. The Tyne at Haydon Bridge reached 4.7m above normal, which is the highest ever recorded. At Corbridge and Haydon Bridge the Tyne burst its banks and 150 residents were evacuated in the early hours of Saturday morning. The River Wear reached highest ever recorded levels at Stanhope.

It was a case of 'water, water everywhere and n'er a drop to drink' in Hexham where the river burst two water mains which resulted in the town being without water. Emergency crews worked in difficult conditions to fix almost two miles of pipes which burst alongside and over the Tyne at Acomb. Up to 10,000 homes, schools and the hospital were without water. People had to use bottled water or fill buckets at emergency bowsers and schools were closed until the water supply was re-connected. Water supplies were also cut off in Allendale and Slaley.

Roofs were ripped off terraced houses in Gateshead and trees were blown down all over the

north, causing much damage. An 88-year-old woman got up to make a cup of tea moments before the chimney of her house crashed onto her bed.

Alston had power cuts and some storm damage but was relatively untouched compared to other regions, though fallen trees caused problems on roads around the town. An RAF helicopter rescued a seriously ill two-year-old girl from town because the ambulance had been unable to get through. The girl was flown to the Cumberland Infirmary.

Crosby-on-Eden, near Carlisle, was badly hit by the floods with 75 per cent of the village's homes under water. The water was about five feet deep and

Flooding at Wetheral, photo. Patricia Howe. Patricia said: 'I was one of the lucky ones - my house is built on a rock 30 feet above the river and the garden bore the brunt of the flood. Six panels of fencing floated away but we managed to rescue them one by one from the river. We lost 25 panes of glass from the greenhouse and most of the contents, including a ten-year-old and much loved fig tree which produced lovely fruit. The shed is a write off and we also lost a lot of soil and all the chipped bark I put in last year.'

Eamont Bridge - at least the ducks are happy!
Photo. Fred Wilson.

also wrecked the Stag Inn, the Meat and Two Veg restaurant, the golf club and the school. Villagers felt forgotten and isolated as the spotlight focussed on Carlisle. The village is on one of the highest risk flood plains in the county.

The torrential rain and rising rivers brought floods to Armathwaite, Warwick Bridge, Wetheral, Kirkoswald and to Lazonby where the bridge was completely under water. At Langwathby the River Eden rose an estimated 25 feet washing away part of the road and the floods swept into nearby Toll Bar Cottage and into the Edenhall Cricket Pavilion. The floods washed away a small truck which had been delivering sandbags, leaving it about 200 metres from the road. The driver escaped without injury. In Toll Bar Cottage Tyrone and Wendy Fletcher and their three children were surrounded by raging flood water. The family spent the night upstairs but by 4am on Saturday morning decided they had had enough. They rang the fire service but the rescue services were unable to get to the house.

Further up river at Bolton Mill near Appleby, the Butterworth family - Graeme and Barbara, their daughters Elizabeth and Sally, and Graeme's father, Mr Chris Butterworth, watched in horror as the flood water rose. Barbara Butterworth's graphic description of the flood when she was interviewed for Radio Cumbria on Saturday morning was a hint of things to come further down river.

The family were concerned that they might lose seven horses in a stable about 150 yards from the house and a herd of beef cattle. The mill was surrounded by five feet of water which was coming through the walls of the building. The family managed to get some possessions upstairs but their main concern was the livestock. It was impossible to get to the stable but they could hear the horses which thankfully survived the floods. Sadly the family's 25 hens were drowned.

The Butterworths run a caravan site and during the night they could hear tremendous bangs and crashes as caravans were ripped from their foundations and sent crashing into each other. Some of the caravans came to rest 150 yards away, some were smashed and possessions were littered across the site. Family, neighbours and friends rallied round after the flood to help with the clear up.

Appleby-in-Westmorland is perhaps more used to floods than any other town in the region as the River Eden snakes around the town centre. The flood warning sounded at 1.30pm on Friday as water levels rose rapidly. Teams of workmen from the Environment Agency arrived to close the floodgates on the Boroughgate side of town which were designed to protect Chapel Street. Teams also filled sandbags in a desperate attempt to stem the flow of water on the Sands. Eden District Council brought some 200 tonnes of sand to the town for sandbags and residents worked to protect their homes.

The water continued to rise through the evening and just after 8pm it began to flood over the sandbag wall and into shops and business premises on the Sands. By 11pm the water was three feet deep on the Sands. At this stage some residents decided to leave their homes and move to higher ground and two people had to be rescued from a shop with life jackets and a life-line because of the powerful flow of the waist deep water.

Eventually the water was about four feet deep. The floods could not drain away fast enough and began to sweep into Bridge Street, High Wiend and Chapel Street. People said later that it was the worst flood

147

The Sands, Appleby, photo., Westmorland Gazette.

anyone could remember.

It was hoped that the floodgates would protect Chapel Street but by the early hours of Saturday morning it became clear that the flood was too great and residents would have to be evacuated. In total about forty people had to rescued by the emergency services from Chapel Street and the Sands.

Emergency services began to evacuate people at around 3am as the water was still rising and by this time it was only two inches from the top of the flood-gates and the barriers were leaking with the pressure of water. Soon after 6am the electricity went off, plunging the town into darkness, and making the sit-uation even more difficult though, by this time, the water had stopped rising.

Mayor of Appleby, Frank Harland, opened the pub-lic hall for residents to take shelter from their flood-ed homes. He said: 'The pressure of the water was so great it was leaking through the joints of the flood barrier. But water also seemed to pour in from high-er up, causing it to flow down Doomgate and into Chapel Street where it flooded homes.'

Mr Harland said: 'Appleby's thoughts go out to those in Carlisle, who suffered a later, greater flooding, as well as those around the Indian Ocean who have suffered an even greater tragedy.'

Local butcher Norman Dowding made bacon sandwiches for those in the public hall who were also served with hot drinks. As morning came residents made their way home to see the extent of the damage left by the flood.

There was plenty of community spirit in the town and on Saturday morning five pupils from Appleby Grammar School - Jay-Jay Iveson, Sarah and Amy Fitton, Aimie Good and Dean Cape - made coffee and tea for residents using a gas cooker. They later received good citizen awards from the town council.

Almost a hundred homes and businesses were affected by the floods. St Lawrence's Church near the cricket pitch did not escape - it was under nearly three feet of water. Services had to be cancelled and there were fears that the newly restored organ could be damaged. The Methodist Chapel on the Sands was also slightly flooded. The Co-op is above the

Warwick Bridge, photo. Anton Hodge.

street level but the flood water inundated the building, leaving the basement and floors sodden and unsafe. Staff served customers from the doorway for a few days until the building was closed for restoration.

Next door at Roy Ashley's Motors garage on the Sands the flood caused more than £100,000 worth of damage. Computer equipment, furniture and fittings were destroyed and the building had some structural damage. Luckily the garage had time to move all the cars before the River Eden burst its banks.

Further up the Eden Valley at Kirkby Stephen, the Eden does not flow as close to the centre of town as in Appleby but the town centre was flooded for the first time that anyone could remember, leaving residents without electricity and, in some cases, without a water supply.

Drains could not cope with the sheer volume of water which began to flood into houses. The situation was made worse by vehicles which continued to drive through the town, causing waves which flooded further into people's homes. Townspeople formed a human road block to divert traffic around the old post office to stop the problem.

In the nearby villages of Crosby Garrett, Soulby, Warcop, Hartley and Great Asby there was also flooding. Local firefighters were called to many places to pump out flooding houses but the water was flowing back into properties as fast as they pumped it out. In North Road, Kirkby Stephen, firefighters spent three hours pumping out a cellar.

Brough was hit by a power cut which lasted the best part of a week. The village shop and the post office were both lit by candles and freezers full of food were lost. Sadly thieves took advantage of the power cut, darkness and lack of alarms, and broke into the village shop, causing around £600 of damage.

There was serious flooding in Eamont Bridge, near Penrith, with two feet of water in some homes. In Penrith the Thacka Beck overflowed causing flooding in Crown Terrace. The Ethel Austin clothes store had about two feet of water but staff managed to stem the flow with sandbags. Some shops were not able to open because staff could not get through the floods while others had a bumper weekend as shoppers from Carlisle and other flooded areas came to buy items like gas stoves, batteries, lanterns, torches and candles. The town's supermarkets also had an exceptional trading day. The George Hotel, like many other hotels in the town, was full of 'refugees' from Carlisle. Between Penrith and Eamont Bridge, the police headquarters at Carleton Hall also suffered some flooding.

On the A66 just to the east of Penrith, around 4,000 holidaymakers were evacuated from the Center Parcs Oasis Whinfell Forest holiday village after all power was lost. The guests were staying in some 700 villas dotted through the forest and were asked to leave on Saturday afternoon. Some of the villas were damaged by falling trees and one or two were flooded. Press officer Simon Kay said it was the first time the village had had to close and that holidaymakers had been offered a return holiday later in the year to compensate.

There was flooding in Newton Reigny, near Penrith, where the Sun Inn had around eighteen inches of water and at Morland some properties were flooded when the beck burst its banks.

There was flooding in many places in the Lake District, including Pooley Bridge and Ullswater which overflowed onto the road along its whole length. Residents of Watermillock were cut off as the road was flooded in both directions and a fallen tree cut power supplies to Glenridding and Patterdale leaving residents with no power for a week.

The Lake District National Park Authority warned people not to go walking in some areas of the Lake District because of storm damage and flooding - bridges were down, trees lay across many paths and there were large craters in some paths where flood water had washed away the surface. At Kentmere 200 tonnes of material was washed from paths and a landslide blocked a bridleway above the Blencathra Centre at Threlkeld. Three bridges were destroyed one near Bassenthwaite Lake, one in Eskdale and another in Langdale. The National Park centre at Brockhole was closed until the end of January because of the number of fallen trees and damage to the building. In Grizedale Forest all routes except the main sculpture trail were closed because of fallen trees.

Nearly 200 residents of streets in the Crosthwaite Road and High Hill areas of Keswick were evacuated and emergency reception centres were set up at

Looking towards Bridge Street, Appleby, photo. Westmorland Gazette.

Keswick School and the Skiddaw Hotel after the River Greta broke its banks. The floods were worst in the western part of the town and residents were evacuated by boat in the early hours of Saturday morning when the water engulfed homes, shops and businesses.

Keswick Mountain Rescue Team were called out to help with the evacuation. They were helped by nine members of the RAF Leeming Mountain Rescue Team who happened to be based in the area over the weekend. The team's boat and four wheel drive vehicles were used to help evacuate around fifty people, including the elderly, children and pets.

A 79-year-old man, Owen Beattie, was an indirect victim of the floods. Mr Beattie was a resident of the Ravensfield Old People's Home at High Hill and collapsed and died while being transferred to hospital in Penrith. In all 28 residents from Ravensfield were evacuated when flood water from the swollen River Greta was lapping at the door.

Fallen trees on the roads around the town made the situation worse. Inspector David Watson of Keswick police praised the 'heroic' efforts of his officers, other emergency service workers and volunteers.

In the northern Lake District, Cockermouth was badly affected by floods when the Rivers Derwent and Cocker both broke their banks. Police helped to rescue twenty families and the main street was closed off. The floods were up to three feet deep in some homes and the town's cricket field was like a lake.

Community spirit

One of the most striking aspects of flood hit Carlisle, was the amazing community spirit as residents helped each other in so many ways. There was a 'Dunkirk' spirit in the city and many people said it was like Britain during the war. Strangers spoke to each other on the street, neighbours who had never spoken got to know each other. People were talking to each other from upstairs windows and, using a system of plastic bags and rope, were sharing useful items such as candles with one another. Many people, like Rebecca David from Wigton Road commented on the change. She said: 'What has surprised me the most is the tremendous community spirit that this has caused. Before this no one would ever talk to someone in the street but now no one seems to care, amazing!'

In a similar vein Richard Goodfellow said: 'I am amazed at the way people have stuck together and helped each other through this horrible time. Like everyone else I am so despondent that this has happened to our town, but if we carry on with the same

Rescue workers on Warwick Road,
photo. Jeff Gibson.

attitude we will have the place back on its feet in no time.'

Student, Mark Mallinson, said: 'Carlisle is a great city and the way it has pulled together to get through this is amazing. It really makes me proud... It was a time to stand up and be counted, and the citizens of Carlisle really did that.'

Residents in other towns across the county, such as Keswick and Appleby, were praised for their community efforts. When floods hit their towns many people volunteered to help the emergency services in the evacuation of people stuck in flooded homes.

At 8.30am on the Saturday morning of the flood Cumbria Ambulance Service asked for Red Cross assistance at the two reception centres in Carlisle. Teams of volunteers came forward to man the centres providing hot drinks, beds and help for members of the public forced to leave their homes. Volunteers came from many areas including Yorkshire and Scotland.

Two emergency refuge centres were set up in the city to look after those who had been evacuated. The centres were at the North Cumbria Technology College in Harraby and the Wigton Road Methodist Church. They were run by around sixty volunteers from the Salvation Army, Red Cross, Women's Royal Voluntary Service and the St. John's Ambulance.

Hundreds of people were given food, blankets and support at the centres until they were able to find places to stay with family or friends. Some people arrived at the reception centres with bare feet, dressed only in their pyjamas and without a single possession. Some needed treatment for cuts and other injuries when they arrived at the reception centres which also provided a home for pets, including dogs, cats and budgies.

Around a hundred people stayed in the centres for longer periods, including pensioners, babies and toddlers. As well as food and blankets, evacuees could also have hot showers and there was a make-shift cinema for entertainment. The evacuees included some residents from two hostels for homeless men on John Street and Bridge Lane.

The community rallied in support of each other with people like Sandra Stephenson from Scotby who said: 'I'm helping out by taking food to friends, trying to get some normality back into their lives.' Photo. Peter Koronka.

Those who had no relatives or friends in the immediate area stayed in the centres for longer. Many students were in this situation and these included students from the Cumbrian Institute of the Arts who spent a few nights at the emergency centre in Harraby. Nineteen-year-old Matthew Gower and 21-year-old Arlo Clyne, both media students, were only alerted to the floods when they rang for a pizza and were told their road was flooded. They did manage to get quite a lot of stuff upstairs and, after more needy neighbours had been rescued, they waded out and abandoned their house. Mr Gower said: 'It was frightening; the water rose quickly. It rose about four feet in an hour.'

The centre at the North Cumbria Technology College was run by Carol Vallely. She said: 'Most people were brought to us by the police and voluntary organisations, though a lot were coming themselves. One of the biggest problems for them was that they were walking in bare feet and wet clothes.

'Some have been separated from their families. There are quite a number of older people who left their medication behind and we tried to help with that. There are also younger people who are students in the area and haven't got anywhere to go on to so they are having to stay here.' Mrs Vallely praised the response to local radio appeals for bedding, soap and toiletries for the evacuees. People had also given toys and books for the children.

Carlisle Housing Association officer, John Little, coordinated the relief effort at the main reception centre at the North Cumbria Technology College. He said: 'This is the worst thing which has happened in this city in my lifetime. We had 150 people in here yesterday and about 60 stayed overnight but we have had about 100 more people who have come in today to register.

'Many of them were evacuated by boat and have lost everything. Some of them came in here in bare feet and we have been doing our best to give them warm food, spare clothes, and a roof over there heads. When we first opened the relief centre there

Pictured left to right, Justin Telford from Carlisle, with Westley Barton, James Morgan and Ian Rainford, all from Lancaster. They were working for Alfred McAlpine laying water pipes through the city centre before the flood hit. As they couldn't work on the project they volunteered to help with the clean up and were pumping out water from cellars in Corporation Road. Photo. Peter Koronka.

was nothing, but all these good Samaritans have come together and we now have a generator and enough food to feed 3,000 people.'

Mr Little said volunteers had provided 2,000 meals for around 300 people by Tuesday, as well as countless hot drinks and sandwiches. He said it had been a brilliant team effort.

The Ukranian Club on Silloth Road stayed open all night to provide soup, hot drinks, blankets and beds for people. It wasn't an official reception centre but steward Paul Bohaczewskyj decided to open the club to help and many people arrived soaking wet and freezing cold. Paul was helped by his wife Kath, mum Kathleen, daughter Anna, former barmaid Claire Jefferson and Carlisle's mayor Cllr Ralph Aldersey. Cllr Geoff Hodgson and his wife Jenny, were also helping. All the emergency reception centres were highly praised for their work.

Norman Street Primary School was turned into a food aid centre to help people in one of the worst hit areas of the city. People could get hot meals, drinks, candles and other essentials from the school. Teachers became dinner ladies to help provide food for people. Hot food was also delivered to people in their homes.

Social services teams were supporting vulnerable residents and the elderly. Local charities such as Shelter, gave clothes to people who had lost everything while the Salvation Army was collecting furniture for flood hit residents. Carlisle Housing Association also helped with the voluntary work. The British Red Cross had 25 volunteers covering the city at any one time - volunteers came from all over the north of England and Scotland. The WRVS had around 30 volunteers from the area helping to run the refuge centres. Carlisle and District Citizens

Fiona Meyer, youth worker and Jean Ranson, children's minister at the Elim Community Church, who were running a refreshments caravan near St. Aidan's Church, photo. Peter Koronka.

Advice Bureau set up a special hotline for help people hit by flooding or power cuts.

The rescue operation and the reception centres could not have run so smoothly if it hadn't been for this army of volunteers many of whom were attached to organisations and charities but a lot were simply members of the public who could not stand by and watch but had to do something to help.

The ladies at the Magpie Pub in Victoria Road showed great community spirit by providing endless cups of tea and coffee and snacks for the rescuers and the rescued on Saturday. They also made up food parcels to be taken out on boats to those stranded in their homes. Many people offered beds in their homes for people made homeless by the floods. Radio Cumbria did an excellent job of letting people know about places to stay. Many stayed in place after the disaster to help with the clean up operation.

Mark Tomlinson helped with the clean up and said: 'What I came across will live with me for the rest of my life. It was utter devastation.'

Lesley Elston, photo. Peter Koronka.

David Morris and James Greensmith were doing voluntary work and were mending a fence which had been washed away by the floods at the bottom of Tilbury Road. They said that it was the older people who were suffering the most and that the flood had brought out the community spirit in people.

Lesley Elston lives on London Road in Carlisle and was one of many ordinary people who did extraordinary things on the day of the flood. She said: 'My friends were away in London and I suddenly realised that no one would be able to get into the house which is in Petteril Street. A student called Davie Lee lodges with them and I had to wake him up and eventually, with his help, we managed to clear all the front room of furniture. We carried it upstairs and wedged it on the landing. The water was slopping against the doors and coming in by then. We couldn't save all the furniture as the water was coming in so fast. Somehow, by the time I came out of the house, I had lost my boots. The house was dry when I first got there and my feet were a bit wet so I took my boots off. I haven't seen them since. By the time I came out of the house the water was up to my thighs. I've been back to the house since and there was stinking thick brown mud everywhere. It's a terrible mess. People have been amazing though and I've heard of one regular Carlisle 'baddy' who has made some heroic rescues.'

A volunteer at one of the emergency reception centres said he had bumped into an old girlfriend he had not seen in 42 years when she was evacuated from her home. Peter Ostle, a retired college lecturer from Rydal Street, was serving hot drinks at the North Cumbrian Technical College when Edna Croft noticed his name badge. The pair met in 1963 when Peter was working at a record shop in Maryport.

They dated for three or four months but when Edna went to college they lost touch. Edna was flooded out of her home in Kingfisher Park and was brought to the centre with her daughter.

People had to flee their homes in other areas of Cumbria. The following story is from the *Cumberland and Westmorland Herald*, 15 January 2005: After spending four days in her home with no power, 94-year-old Peggie Tweddell decided she needed to find somewhere to stay. She couldn't find an old peoples' home able to take her so she rang the

The Salvation Army Emergency Response vehicle providing refreshments in Warwick Road. Pictured, left to right, Major Mel Robinson from Carlisle, Jennifer and Lawrence Heaton from Penrith, and roofers Jim McLeish and John Hughes. Major Robinson said: 'I've been here since day one. I was called in for the reception centre at Harraby and then moved down to Norman Street School and then onto the community centre where we have been giving people pastoral support, clothes and toiletries.' Photo. Peter Koronka.

The Salvation Army bus outside Carlisle United's shop. Pictured, left to right, front - Linda Elliott, Marjorie Hirst, both from Carlisle, and Sheila Boyes from Low Hesket. Middle row - Stuart Mallin, Stella Board and Vera Forster, all from Carlisle. Standing at the back Jim Taylor from Gainsborough, who drives the bus. He said: 'I got a telephone call on Wednesday to ask if I could come to help. I was going to Romania but I came here instead. We are just providing a warm place for people to sit and talk. We're also doing some refreshments such as soup, pies and pasties. Photo. Peter Koronka.

nearby world-renowned Sharrow Bay Hotel and the manager arrived in a four wheel drive to drive her through the floods to stay at the hotel.

Quite a number of volunteers were working under the Churches Together and Pray for the City organisations. Carlisle churches and the Salvation Army joined together to form the Carlisle Churches' Flood Response Team. They were helping people clean up their properties, doing washing and ironing for residents, providing hot food and refreshments, a listening ear, house

View down Church Street, photo. David Jamison.

sitting and transport, photograph restoration and someone to pray with. They had a caravan outside St Aidan's Church, another at the Carlisle United shop on Warwick Road and there was also a Salvation Army emergency bus travelling the area.

Youth worker Fiona Meyer said: 'A lot of churches have come together in the city and they have been doing all sorts of different things to help people. We are doing teas, coffees, pies and food for residents, contractors and workmen. We can also sit and chat for a bit if people need to talk. The Salvation Army have supplied a lot of the food but people and businesses have been really generous.'

The aftermath

Perhaps the most distressing time was when people returned to their flood damaged homes. In the shock and hurry of being evacuated the full implications of the flood may not have sunk in. But when people returned to their homes to see photographs, family heirlooms, old books, student dissertations - things which were impossible or difficult to replace - ruined by the filthy brown flood water then the full horror became apparent.

People broke down in tears when they saw the damage but then most rallied around when they were able to put things in perspective, especially when they remembered those who had lost their lives.

Health officials warned people that they could catch diseases if they did not wear protective clothing while they cleaned up flood damaged homes. The flood water could have been contaminated with sewage, oil, petrol or other hazardous chemicals, which was why so many things had to be thrown away.

Furniture and carpets were piled up on the streets for the bin men to take away - it was a sad sight. The clean up would take many months and a huge

Corporation Road, photo. Peter Koronka.

amount of money.

Carlisle Mind warned that people might begin to feel isolated, disorientated and over-stressed after the disaster, especially when they realised the personal implications of what had happened.

Teams of cleaners and contractors were soon leafleting the area and a police spokesman said some of these gangs were unscrupulous. Cumbria Country Council Trading Standards were also warning house-holders to be on the look out for bogus property repairers cashing in on people desperate to repair their homes. The department received complaints and enquiries from city residents after con men were out knocking at doors. Head of Trading Standards, Phil Ashcroft, said: 'I am extremely sorry to have to warn the public that the bogey men are out and about looking to cash in on the misery and desperation to get roofing and other repair work done.'

The Environment Agency held 'drop-in' surgeries in towns across the county for people affected by the flooding. The agency wanted to hear peoples' experiences to help them plan future flood defences and were also offering people advice.

The insurance bill for damage to Carlisle alone was put at over £50 million and sadly some reports sug-

Warwick Road - by Monday morning people had started putting their ruined carpets and furniture out onto the street, photo. Peter Koronka.

gested that up to one in four households affected by the floods were not covered by insurance. Some people said they could not afford insurance because of high excess payments in areas prone to flooding.

Many people were waiting for insurance assessors to visit and had been told not to move anything until the damage had been assessed. Royal and Sun Alliance set up a mobile office near Tesco's and North West manager Darren Marshall and East Scotland manager Richard Fairbank were in the city from Sunday morning to help people.

Darren Marshall and Richard Fairbank from Royal & Sun Alliance, photo. Peter Koronka.

Warwick Road, photo. Peter Koronka.

Insurers Norwich Union had a temporary office in the city for anyone affected by the flooding and Halifax Home Insurance drafted in workmen to help with repairs to flood damaged homes.

Some people were not able to start the clean up immediately because they had been advised by their insurance companies to leave everything until an assessor had visited and in some cases people had to wait up to a week in ruined homes without electricity for an assessor's visit.

Prince Charles flew into the city to meet people whose homes were flooded on Friday, 14 January. The Prince, who was one of the first to make a dona-tion to the flood recovery appeal, met residents in Warwick Road and talked to them about their suffering and the cost of restoring their homes. He also visited the police and fire stations in Rickergate and was introduced to some heroic policemen who risked their lives to save others. He met four firemen, including David Pigney, from Appleby, who had been involved in rescuing people during the floods. The Prince also met Cumbria County Council leader Tim Stoddard, from Kirkby Stephen, who told the Prince about the fantastic community spirit during the crisis.

The Cumbria Community Foundation's Flood

Warwick Road, photo. Peter Koronka.

Relief Recovery Appeal was launched immediately after the disaster with £50,000 of its own money and raised £250,000 in just four days with donations coming in from Cumbria, all across the country and from overseas.

Generous donations came from business including accountants Dodd & Co, British Nuclear Fuels, Cumbrian Newspapers, Carrs Milling Industries, Nestlé and the Kingmoor Park Charitable Trust, which pledged £50,000. Cumbria County Council also put in £50,000 and Rural Regeneration Cumbria gave £25,000. Other donations came from United Utilities, HSBC Bank, West Bromwich Building Society and Keswick Lions. Asda stores nationwide were collecting for the appeal.

The Foundation, which is based in Cockermouth, aimed to raise £500,000 and the money was given to those who suffered financial hardship because of the floods and to voluntary and community groups.

Andrew Beeforth, director of the Cumbria Community Foundation, said: 'The response from local companies and development agencies has been tremendous. We are also starting to receive money from the general public as well.'

The Cumbria Flood Recovery Fund appeal continued to gather momentum and the committee were soon handing

All along the streets there were piles of ruined possessions, with precious photographs, videos, family heirlooms and many irreplaceable items being thrown onto lorries and into skips, photos. Peter Koronka.

out money.

'We are delighted that we have been able to support so many excellent projects so soon,' said Susan Aglionby, chair of the committee. 'It is a credit to church and voluntary groups that they have responded so quickly to the needs of people affected by the storms.'

Grants were allocated to voluntary and community groups providing support to people affected by the storms and to individuals and families to help with food, clothing, heating, heating equipment, bedding and for some emergency repairs.

Some of the groups which received grants were:

◆ Impact Housing's Centre 47 in Carlisle and Home Appliances in Workington. The projects worked together to recycle donated furniture and white goods and provided them free of charge to people affected by the floods.

◆ The Carlisle Community Law Centre and Carlisle Citizens Advice Bureau, who worked together to provide additional information and advice services including a mobile centre based at areas worst hit by flooding.

◆ Carlisle Churches Flood Response for the valuable relief services they ran in six centres in Carlisle and for their phone service which offered emotional support.

◆ Eden Citizens Advice Bureau who provided an additional weekly session in Appleby to support local people affected by the floods and storms.

◆ Rainbow Soft Play at Carlisle City Church for free play sessions and hot food and drink to families affected by the flood.

◆ Early Birds Breakfast Club at Petteril Bank School who lost all their equipment that was in storage at Bitts Park whilst building work was being

Victoria Place, photo. Peter Koronka.

undertaken at the school.

'It's great that we are getting money out where it is needed so quickly,' said Andrew Beeforth, Director of the Community Foundation, 'but the number of applications we are receiving is giving us a clear picture of just what need is out there. We must keep raising funds if we are to be able respond to everyone'.

The flood recovery fund received donations and

Photos. Peter Longworth.

messages of goodwill from all over the country. Just a few of these are listed below:

Mrs Potter from Loughborough who sent £104.15, made up from collections at the canteen, shop floor, outside hauliers, two children who gave 50p each and around £20 in coppers from the 'sweet fund', plus £5 from her neighbour.

Mr Stacey from Suffolk sent £10. His mother was born in Stanwix and his father lived in Richardson Street. He had seen the news reports and said: 'It is only £10 but as a pensioner it is all I can manage at this time but send it with heartfelt sympathy for all who have suffered in this catastrophe.'

Mrs Hewitson from Workington sent two cheques for £50 and £100. She said: 'My dad and I are both pensioners, but would like to help with your appeal'.

Mrs Cunningham from Berwickshire sent £20 and said: 'Please give to older residents, particularly a lady seen on ITV who is 98 years old.'

Mrs Purdy from Sussex also sent £20 and said: 'As I made a small donation to the tsunami

167

Victoria Place, photo. Peter Koronka.

disaster, I feel it incumbent on me to make a similar one to my own country folk, particularly as I have a deep affection for Cumbria.'

Mrs Richardson from High Wycome sent £50. She said: 'I come from Barrow and regularly go home for visits and to research my family history. My thoughts are with you all.'

Rene Barber from Whitehaven sent £50 and said: 'If you need any help unstuffing envelopes or answering the phone give me a yell.'

A donation was also sent from the people of Boscastle who held a dance to support the fund. They knew how the residents of Carlisle felt and wanted to help.

Miss S Allan who did not send an address sent £300 'for dear, brave Carlisle.'

Jaybeam employees in Wellingborough collected £105 and said: 'This was raised from employees who donated money at Christmas instead of sending cards to each other.'

A lady from Torquay sent £20, 'her weekly income' to help 'a mother with all the extra stress of keeping her family together when there is no home.'

As this book went to print the Cumbria Flood Recovery Fund had raised £540,000.